RICHARD
McGUIRE

———

THEN
AND THERE,
HERE
AND NOW

CARTOONMUSEUM BASEL
Zentrum für narrative Kunst
Centre for Narrative Art (Hg./ed.)

RICHARD
McGUIRE

THEN
AND THERE,
HERE
AND NOW

CHRISTOPH MERIAN VERLAG

EN

In a career spanning more than 40 years, the illustrator, designer and artist Richard McGuire of the USA, born in 1957, has explored and experimented in many artistic disciplines, whereby illustration and comics have an important place in his wide-ranging output. With his graphic novel *Here*, published in 2014, McGuire created a book that is rightly regarded as a significant driving force for comics. The 300-page graphic novel, which is being adapted into a feature film, jumbles up the past, present and future of our planet in one small place. *Here* is an ode to life in the form of a dizzying narrative, characterized by cleverly simplified aesthetics and a minimalist language of forms: Set in a living room based on the one in his family home, *Here* lets us travel through billions of years as if in a time machine – from the first appearance of life on Earth, past the moment when the house and its living room are standing, and into the distant future. The basis for the graphic novel was a short six-page comic strip that McGuire had published back in 1989, in Art Spiegelman and Françoise Mouly's comic magazine *RAW*. In 2016, the graphic novel, which has since been translated into 20 languages, was awarded the Fauve d'or, the highest French accolade for graphic novels.

As McGuire's most comic-related work, *Here* became the starting point for the conception of a retrospective dedicated to the artist at Cartoonmuseum Basel: *Then and There, Here and Now*, which has in turn given rise to this publication based on it. The exhibition presents McGuire's beginnings as a street artist whose stencil drawings were seen in 1980s New York, as well as his time as bassist and co-founder of the pioneering post-punk band Liquid Liquid, for which he created a much-sampled iconic bass line. The spectrum extends from illustrations and covers for *The New Yorker*, which he worked on after the band broke up, to children's books and toys, through to animations that he designed and directed, and originals – for his key work *Here* and for a current, as yet untitled graphic novel that will merge visual art with music.

This book is the enthralling and vital essence of an artistic development that never rests and, driven by creative curiosity, constantly opens doors for itself. The publication presents a body of work that, despite its enormous breadth, also has many constants and internal references. It is therefore

DE

In seiner über 40-jährigen Karriere hat der 1957 geborene US-amerikanische Zeichner, Designer und Künstler Richard McGuire sich forschend und experimentierend durch viele künstlerische Disziplinen bewegt, wobei Illustration und Comic in diesem breitgefächerten Werk einen wichtigen Platz einnehmen. Mit seiner 2014 erschienenen Graphic Novel ‹Hier› hat McGuire ein Buch geschaffen, das zu Recht als bedeutender Impulsgeber für den Comic gilt. Die 300-seitige Graphic Novel, die aktuell verfilmt wird, wirbelt Vergangenheit, Gegenwart und Zukunft unseres Planeten an einem kleinen Ort durcheinander. ‹Hier› ist eine Ode an das Leben in Form einer schwindelerregenden Erzählung, die sich durch eine raffiniert vereinfachte Ästhetik und eine minimalistische Formensprache auszeichnet: In einem an McGuires Elternhaus angelehnten Wohnraum lässt ‹Hier› uns wie in einer Zeitmaschine durch Milliarden von Jahren reisen – vom Erscheinen des Lebens auf der Erde vorbei am Moment, in dem das Haus und sein Wohnzimmer stehen, bis in die ferne Zukunft. Grundlage für die Graphic Novel war eine sechsseitige Kurzgeschichte, die McGuire bereits 1989 im Comicmagazin ‹RAW› von Art Spiegelman und Françoise Mouly veröffentlicht hatte. Im Jahr 2016 wurde die inzwischen in 20 Sprachen übersetzte Graphic Novel mit dem Fauve d'or geehrt, der höchsten französischen Auszeichnung für Graphic Novels.

Als das dem Comic verwandteste Werk von McGuire wurde ‹Hier› zum Ausgangspunkt der Konzeption der 2024 dem Künstler gewidmeten Retrospektive ‹Then and There, Here and Now› im Cartoonmuseum Basel, die wiederum Anlass und Grundlage ist für diese Publikation. Die Ausstellung zeigt die Anfänge McGuires als Street-Art-Künstler, dessen Schablonenzeichnungen im New York der 1980er-Jahre zu sehen waren, sowie seine Zeit als Bassist und Mitgründer der bahnbrechenden Post-Punk-Band Liquid Liquid, für die er einen vielgesampelten, ikonischen Basslauf kreierte. Der Bogen reicht von Illustrationen und Titelseiten für ‹The New Yorker›, mit denen er sich nach Auflösung der Band beschäftigte, über Kinderbücher und Spielsachen bis hin zu Animationsfilmen, die er konzipierte und bei denen er Regie führte, und weiter zu Originalen für sein Schlüsselwerk ‹Hier› sowie für eine aktuelle, noch namenlose Graphic Novel, die bildende Kunst und Musik fusionieren wird.

no surprise that certain aspects can be found throughout his œuvre, from its beginnings to the present day. McGuire started out at the interface between sound and image, and now his latest works bring these two sensory impressions together again: There is *Listen*, a book created in the wake of the isolation caused by the corona pandemic, which gives graphic form to sounds around McGuire's house north of New York City. There are also the sound drawings created in recent years, which act as a kind of notation created by McGuire, as well as works for a graphic novel that will look into the meaning of sounds.

The exhibition and this publication show McGuire's output as an inherently round but open circle, as evidence of a searching personality who is interwoven with his time and his companions, yet simultaneously creates on a basis of immense independence. The exhibition and publication would not have been possible if it had not been for McGuire making his work available, and supporting the participants with important input and insight. Vincent Tuset-Anrès, general and artistic director of Fotokino in Marseille, developed this publication in cooperation with McGuire. I wholeheartedly thank both of them for their generous and patient involvement, which provided fertile ground for the exhibition at Cartoonmuseum Basel to grow on. My visit to a small McGuire exhibition at Studio Fotokino in 2021 was what prompted me to delve deeper into this artist's work. I am delighted with the manifold results that have since emerged from the fruitful collaboration between McGuire, Fotokino and Cartoonmuseum Basel. A big thank-you also goes to Oliver Bolanz and his team at Christoph Merian Verlag, for their enthusiastic support of this project.

    Anette Gehrig
    Director and curator, Cartoonmuseum Basel –
    Centre for Narrative Art

Das Buch ist die packende und vitale Essenz einer künstlerischen Entwicklung, die niemals ruht und sich, getrieben von kreativer Neugier, ständig selbst Türen öffnet. Es stellt ein Werk vor, das trotz seiner enormen Breite auch viele Konstanten und innere Bezüge aufweist. So ist es auch nicht verwunderlich, dass sich gewisse Aspekte in seinem gesamten Werk wiederfinden, von den Anfängen bis hin in die Gegenwart. McGuire ist an der Schnittstelle von Klang und Bild gestartet, und nun bringen aktuelle Arbeiten diese beiden Sinneseindrücke wieder zusammen. Da ist ‹Listen›, ein in der Folge der Isolation durch die Corona-Pandemie entstandenes Buch, das Geräuschen um McGuires Haus nördlich von New York City eine grafische Gestalt verleiht. Und da sind die in den letzten Jahren geschaffenen Klangzeichnungen, die wie eine von McGuire kreierte Notation funktionieren, sowie Arbeiten für eine Graphic Novel, die der Bedeutung von Klängen nachgehen wird.

Die Ausstellung und die vorliegende Publikation zeigen McGuires Werk als in sich runden, aber offenen Kreis, als Zeuge einer suchenden Persönlichkeit, die mit ihrer Zeit sowie ihren Begleiter:innen verwoben ist und gleichzeitig aus einer tiefen Eigenständigkeit schöpft. Ausstellung und Publikation konnten nur zustande kommen, weil McGuire sein Werk zur Verfügung stellte und die Beteiligten mit wichtigen Impulsen und Einsichten unterstützte. Vincent Tuset-Anrès, Direktor und künstlerischer Leiter von Fotokino in Marseille, hat in Zusammenarbeit mit McGuire die Publikation erarbeitet. Beiden danke ich herzlich für ihr grosszügiges, geduldiges Engagement, auf dessen Boden auch die Ausstellung im Cartoonmuseum Basel wachsen konnte. Der Besuch einer kleinen Ausstellung von McGuire im Studio Fotokino war 2021 für mich der Impuls, tiefer in das Werk des Künstlers einzutauchen, und ich freue mich sehr über die vielfältigen Früchte, die die seither gediehene Kollaboration zwischen McGuire, Fotokino und Cartoonmuseum Basel trägt. Ein grosser Dank geht auch an Oliver Bolanz und sein Team vom Christoph Merian Verlag, die dieses Projekt mit Begeisterung mitgetragen haben.

    Anette Gehrig
    Direktorin und Kuratorin, Cartoonmuseum Basel –
    Zentrum für narrative Kunst

1980

THEN AND THERE, HERE AND NOW

Born in New Jersey in 1957, Richard McGuire studied art at Rutgers University in New Brunswick, some 60 kilometers from New York City. "I was regularly between the two cities, as I sometimes worked in galleries during my studies," he says. "Of course, I couldn't escape the graffiti that covered the subway trains. The art scene at the time consisted mainly of conceptual and performance art, and it didn't seem as exciting as what was happening in the streets."

While still in college in the late 1970s, McGuire formed Liquid Idiot, the precursor to Liquid Liquid. "Our music was naïve, something akin to outsider art," McGuire says. The band's name "came from two words drawn at random from a hat, and it suited what we were doing." There was also an expanded iteration of the band, known as The Idiot Orchestra, "with 12 of us on stage" playing a variety of instruments including violin, trumpet, and marimba.

In July of 1979, at the age of 22, he moved to New York City and immersed himself in the downtown art scene, where musicians, visual artists, poets, performers, and filmmakers mingled and moved from one medium to another without restraint. By August, Liquid Idiot had played its first show at the iconic CBGB. The band quickly found its place among a myriad of New York-based artists such as DNA, ESG, Y Pants, Glenn Branca, and Sonic Youth.

McGuire was also focused on an art project, which he'd begun during his first week in the city. "I started making stencil drawings, using spray paint and crayon, of a character named Ixnae Nix," he says. The character's vague human silhouette was partially inspired by petroglyphs he'd seen in caves just a few years earlier while on a road trip through New Mexico. Its name is a double negation – *ixnae* being pig Latin for *nix*, or nothing. To create the

Richard McGuire wurde 1957 in New Jersey geboren und studierte Kunst an der Rutgers University in New Brunswick, etwa 60 Kilometer von New York City entfernt. «Ich pendelte regelmässig zwischen den beiden Städten, da ich während meines Studiums manchmal in Galerien arbeitete», erinnert er sich. «Natürlich konnte ich dabei die Graffitis auf den U-Bahnen nicht übersehen. Die Kunstszene bestand damals hauptsächlich aus Konzept- und Performancekunst, aber was sich auf den Strassen abspielte, kam mir viel aufregender vor.»

Noch während seines Studiums gründete McGuire in den späten 1970er-Jahren Liquid Idiot, den Vorläufer von Liquid Liquid. «Unsere Musik war naiv, so etwas wie Aussenseiterkunst», sagt McGuire. Der Name der Band «entstand aus zwei zufällig aus einem Hut gezogenen Wörtern, und er passte zu dem, was wir taten». Es gab auch eine erweiterte Version der Band, bekannt als The Idiot Orchestra, «mit zwölf von uns auf der Bühne», die eine Vielzahl von Instrumenten spielten, darunter Violine, Trompete und Marimba.

Im Juli 1979, im Alter von 22 Jahren, zog er nach New York City und tauchte in den Kunstbetrieb der Innenstadt ein, in dem sich Leute aus der Musik-, der Lyrik-, der Film- sowie der darstellenden und bildenden Kunstszene mischten und ohne Einschränkungen von einem Medium zum anderen wechselten. Im August spielten Liquid Idiot ihr erstes Konzert im legendären CBGB. Die Band reihte sich schnell in eine Vielzahl von New Yorker Musikschaffenden ein, wie DNA, ESG, Y Pants, Glenn Branca und Sonic Youth.

Daneben beschäftigte sich McGuire auch mit einem Kunstprojekt, das er in seiner ersten Woche in der Metropole begonnen hatte. «Ich habe angefangen, mit Sprühfarbe und Wachskreide Schablonenzeichnungen einer Figur namens Ixnae

Liquid Liquid, 1980. Scott Hartley, Richard McGuire, Dennis Young, Sal Principato (left to right / von links nach rechts). Photo/Foto: Kishi Yamamoto.

works, he tore the silhouette from large sheets of newspaper, and added to the composition with scraps of sentences written in the manner of poetic and absurd headlines ('Through My Open Mouth'; 'Someone No One Remembers Who'; 'Incident Instantly Becomes Memory') then wheat-pasted the drawings onto the walls of buildings in Lower Manhattan.

"What I was doing wasn't graffiti, but it was a response to graffiti," McGuire says. "Each drawing is like an episode in a series. I made two copies of each, pasting one in the street and keeping the other for my archives. The following day, the work would be photographed by my friend, Martha Fishkin, to document it."

He was also designing posters for his band. He often pasted them up on the same night as the Ixnae Nix drawings. Unlike those images, the band posters were mainly collaged images using hand-drawn type or Letraset, then offset-printed or silkscreened in runs of a hundred or so. Other artists at the time were also drawing on graffiti culture, including Jean-Michel Basquiat and Al Diaz, who worked together as SAMO©. "To me, they were the manifestation of a very powerful, new voice." And Keith Haring, too, who was just beginning to draw his characters on vacant advertising spaces inside New York City subway cars and on station platforms.

Nix anzufertigen», erklärt er. Inspiration für die vage menschliche Silhouette der Figur waren unter anderem Felszeichnungen, die McGuire ein paar Jahre zuvor auf einem Roadtrip durch New Mexico in Höhlen gesehen hatte. Der Name ist eine doppelte Verneinung: *Ixnae* bedeutet in der Spielsprache ‹Pig Latin› (Schweinelatein) dasselbe wie *nix*, also nichts. Für die Arbeiten riss er die Silhouette aus grossen Zeitungsblättern und ergänzte die Komposition durch Satzfetzen, die er im Stil poetisch-absurder Schlagzeilen verfasste, wie ‹Through My Open Mouth› (Durch meinen offenen Mund), ‹Someone No One Remembers Who› (Jemand, an den sich niemand erinnert) oder ‹Incident Instantly Becomes Memory› (Vorfall wird sofort zur Erinnerung). Die fertigen Werke klebte er mit Weizenpaste an Gebäudewände in Lower Manhattan.

«Was ich damals gemacht habe, war kein Graffiti, aber es war eine Reaktion auf Graffiti», erzählt McGuire. «Jedes Bild ist wie eine Folge in einer Serie. Ich fertigte jeweils zwei Kopien an, von denen ich die eine in den Strassen hinklebte, während ich die andere für mein Archiv aufbewahrte. Am Tag danach fotografierte eine Freundin, Martha Fishkin, dann das Werk, um es zu dokumentieren.»

McGuire entwarf auch Plakate für seine Band und brachte sie oft in derselben Nacht an wie die Ixnae-Nix-Bilder. Im Gegensatz zu letzteren waren die Bandplakate hauptsächlich Collagen,

New York / New Wave, PS1, Queens, 1981. (Richard McGuire's Ixnae Nix works, lower right / Richard McGuires Ixnae-Nix-Arbeiten unten rechts). Photo/Foto: Helaine Messer. MoMA PS1 Archives/Archiv, III.A18. The Museum of Modern Art Archives / Archiv des Museum of Modern Art, New York.

Common interests and concerns sparked friendships. McGuire's band shared the bill with Basquiat's band, Gray, at the downtown loft space A's, and Haring invited McGuire to be in exhibitions he put together at Club 57 and The Mudd Club. In 1981, Basquiat, Haring, and McGuire were included in New York / New Wave, an exhibition staged in Queens, New York, at P.S.1, now MoMA PS1, an outpost of the Museum of Modern Art. Other artists represented in the show included Robert Mapplethorpe, Nan Goldin, Ray Johnson, Larry Clark, David Byrne, Laurence Weiner, and William Burroughs.

"I felt that this exhibition was a major event, and I was very happy to be part of it," McGuire says. "The curator, Diego Cortez, had selected around 150 artists, taking the temperature of everything that was happening in the city at the time."

He exhibited at Franklin Furnace the following year. Founded in New York City in 1976 with a focus on books by emerging avant-garde artists, the organization is known today for introducing the early work of Laurie Anderson, Vito Acconci, and Jenny Holzer, among others. McGuire interned there while in college and was later hired as a gallery assistant. Given the opportunity to present work in the gallery's window as part of a group show, he created a large-scale sculptural piece entitled Big Man out the Window. Keith Haring brought

für die er handgezeichnete Schriften oder Letraset-Abreibebuchstaben verwendete und die dann im Offset- oder Siebdruckverfahren in einer Auflage von etwa hundert Stück gedruckt wurden. Auch andere Kunstschaffende griffen zu dieser Zeit auf die Graffiti-Kultur zurück, darunter Jean-Michel Basquiat und Al Diaz, die gemeinsam als SAMO© arbeiteten und von denen McGuire meinte: «Für mich waren sie die Manifestation einer sehr starken, neuen Stimme.» So auch Keith Haring, der damals gerade begann, seine Figuren auf freie Werbeflächen in New Yorker U-Bahn-Wagen und auf Bahnsteigen zu zeichnen.

Gemeinsame Interessen und Anliegen liessen Freundschaften entstehen. McGuires Band trat gemeinsam mit Basquiats Band Gray im Downtown-Loft A's auf, und Haring lud McGuire ein, an den von ihm organisierten Ausstellungen im Club 57 und im Mudd Club teilzunehmen. 1981 nahmen Basquiat, Haring und McGuire an der Ausstellung ‹New York / New Wave› (New York / Neue Welle) teil, die in Queens, New York, im P.S.1 stattfand, dem heutigen MoMA PS1, einer Aussenstelle des Museum of Modern Art. Weiter in der Ausstellung vertreten waren Robert Mapplethorpe, Nan Goldin, Ray Johnson, Larry Clark, David Byrne, Laurence Weiner und William Burroughs.

«Ich fühlte, dass diese Ausstellung ein grosses Ereignis war, und freute mich sehr, dass ich daran

the influential gallery owner Tony Shafrazi to the opening, and McGuire says Shafrazi "offered me a show on the spot." He accepted, and quickly created new work for the exhibition, which opened two months later, on March 27, 1982.

Shortly thereafter, Liquid Liquid set off on its first European tour and when they returned, the band went into the studio to record their third EP, *Optimo*, released in 1983. It is wildly energetic, with a flagship track, *Cavern*, that was popular in the clubs. The song was also getting radio play. Sugar Hill Records and Grandmaster Flash took note, appropriating McGuire's signature bass groove on a new single of their own – *White Lines* – with lyrics by rapper Melle Mel. The track was a hit, and the band's label, 99 Records, was plunged into a legal battle from which it would never recover, and Liquid Liquid disbanded.

Over the years, however, Liquid Liquid developed a cult following. Original records started fetching high prices on auction websites, and bootlegs were popping up. In 1997, the band's complete catalog was reissued in the U.S. by the Beastie Boys on their Grand Royal label, and simultaneously in the U.K.

teilnehmen konnte», schildert McGuire. «Der Kurator Diego Cortez hatte rund 150 Kunstschaffende ausgewählt und so die Stimmung dessen, was zu jener Zeit in der Stadt gerade so geschah, voll eingefangen.»

Im folgenden Jahr stellte McGuire bei Franklin Furnace aus. Die 1976 in New York City gegründete Organisation, deren Schwerpunkt auf Büchern von aufstrebenden Avantgarde-Kunstschaffenden lag, ist heute dafür bekannt, dass sie unter anderem das Frühwerk von Laurie Anderson, Vito Acconci und Jenny Holzer zeigte. McGuire absolvierte dort während seines Studiums ein Praktikum und wurde später als Galerieassistent eingestellt. Als er die Gelegenheit erhielt, im Rahmen einer Gruppenausstellung Arbeiten im Schaufenster der Galerie zu präsentieren, schuf er eine grossformatige skulpturale Arbeit mit dem Titel ‹Big Man out the Window› (Grosser Mann durch das Fenster). Keith Haring brachte den einflussreichen Galeristen Tony Shafrazi zur Vernissage mit, der ihm, so McGuire, «auf der Stelle eine Ausstellung anbot». McGuire sagte zu und schuf in kürzester Zeit neue Arbeiten für die Ausstellung, die bereits zwei Monate später, am 27. März 1982, eröffnet wurde.

Big Man out the Window, 1981. Franklin Furnace, New York, Jan. 1982. Photo/Foto: Franklin Furnace, New York.

Kurz darauf begaben sich Liquid Liquid auf ihre erste Europatournee. Nach ihrer Rückkehr nahmen sie im Studio ihre dritte EP, ‹Optimo›, auf, die 1983 erschien. Die äusserst energiegeladene EP enthält den bekannten Track ‹Cavern› (Höhle), der in den damaligen Clubs sehr beliebt war und auch im Radio gespielt wurde. Sugar Hill Records und Grandmaster Flash wurden auf den Song aufmerksam und übernahmen McGuires charakteristischen Bass-Groove für ihre eigene neue Single ‹White Lines› (Weisse Linien) mit einem Text des Rappers Melle Mel. Der Song war ein Hit, worauf 99 Records, das Label von Liquid Liquid, in einen Rechtsstreit verwickelt wurde, von dem es sich nie mehr erholte und der schliesslich auch zur Auflösung von Liquid Liquid führte.

Im Laufe der Jahre entwickelten Liquid Liquid jedoch eine kultige Anhängerschaft. Die Originalplatten erzielten hohe Preise auf Auktions-Websites und es tauchten immer mehr Bootlegs auf. 1997 wurde der gesamte Katalog der Band in den USA von den Beastie Boys auf ihrem Label Grand Royal und gleichzeitig in Grossbritannien von Mo' Wax neu aufgelegt.

Liquid Liquid, Barbican Hall, London, England. Oct./Okt. 4, 2008. Photo/Foto: unknown/unbekannt.

by Mo' Wax. A series of remixes by various artists soon followed. Before long, McGuire says, "we started getting offers to play in front of thousands of people." The band toured Japan and performed in Germany and France. They played the Montreux Jazz Festival, in Switzerland; and Primavera Sound, in Spain. In 2009, they headlined at New York's Lincoln Center and at the Barbican Centre, in London. In 2010, Liquid Liquid appeared on *The Tonight Show Starring Jimmy Fallon*, playing *Cavern* alongside the show's house band, the Roots, led by Questlove. And in 2011, Liquid Liquid performed in front of nearly 20,000 people as the opening act for LCD Soundsystem at New York's Madison Square Garden.

It was a trajectory McGuire could never have imagined. "After leaving the band [at 25], I wanted to devote myself to my personal work. I always considered myself more of an artist, but I also had to earn a living."

First, in 1983, came the opportunity to create the music for a fashion show for WilliWear, by streetwear pioneer Willi Smith, where McGuire's original composition was accompanied by video art by Nam June Paik. Then came a steady gig at a production company making sets and props, mainly for TV commercials. "I had studied sculpture at Rutgers, so I was familiar with a range of tools and techniques," McGuire says. Computer graphics were still in their infancy, so custom-made props were often used. "If the ad was for a wristwatch, for example, we'd build a large-format version so we

Bald darauf folgte eine Reihe von Remixen durch verschiedene Musikschaffende. Schon bald, fügt McGuire an, «bekamen wir Angebote, vor Tausenden von Menschen zu spielen». Die Band tourte durch Japan und hatte Auftritte in Deutschland sowie Frankreich. Sie spielten auf dem Montreux Jazz Festival in der Schweiz und auf dem Primavera Sound in Spanien. Im Jahr 2009 traten sie als Headliner im New Yorker Lincoln Center sowie im Barbican Centre in London auf. 2010 nahmen Liquid Liquid an der US-amerikanischen Fernsehsendung ‹The Tonight Show Starring Jimmy Fallon› teil, wo sie zusammen mit der Hausband der Show, den Roots, unter der Leitung von Questlove ‹Cavern› performten. Und 2011 spielten Liquid Liquid vor fast 20.000 Menschen als Vorgruppe von LCD Soundsystem im New Yorker Madison Square Garden.

Es war eine Entwicklung, wie McGuire sie sich nie hätte vorstellen können. «Nachdem ich die Band [mit 25] verlassen hatte, wollte ich mich meiner persönlichen Arbeit widmen. Ich habe mich immer mehr als Künstler gesehen, aber ich musste auch meinen Lebensunterhalt verdienen.»

Zunächst bot sich ihm 1983 die Gelegenheit, die Musik für eine Modenschau von WilliWear, dem Label des Streetwear-Pioniers Willi Smith, zu schaffen, bei der McGuires Eigenkomposition von Videokunst von Nam June Paik begleitet wurde. Dann folgte ein fester Job bei einer Produktionsfirma, die – hauptsächlich für Fernsehwerbung – Kulissen und Requisiten herstellte.

could light it properly during the shoot. If it called for a moonscape, we'd create one. A burning tree in the desert? No problem. I was very interested in cinema and the job was a way of getting closer to it and understanding the medium better."

The job also opened a door. "At one point, I worked on a commercial that used animation in combination with three-dimensional backgrounds that I designed and built. The company making the animation seemed more fun, so I convinced them to hire me." They were also producing Pee-wee Herman's TV series, *Pee-wee's Playhouse*, with art direction by Gary Panter. "It was a wild time," McGuire adds, "with a lot of artists and musicians involved in the project."

It was at the animation company that he worked alongside a freelancer, who also happened to be an illustrator. "I admired the fact that he had more control of his time. I was envious!" McGuire says. "I asked him how he got started." After that, "I built up a portfolio and started getting commissions from *The New York Times*, the *Village Voice*, and, eventually, *The New Yorker*."

This steady stream of illustration work enabled McGuire to leave the animation studio and pursue new projects. In the late 1980s, he attended a series of lectures by Art Spiegelman, who would go on to win a Pulitzer Prize for his graphic novel, *Maus*. "In one of his lectures, [Spiegelman] spoke about comics as 'narrative diagrams'," McGuire says. "The word 'diagram' resonated with me."

"I'd just moved into a new apartment and I was thinking about the person who'd lived there before me, and the person before her, and it gave me an idea for something that I thought could be interesting. I had the idea of telling the story of this place as a screen split by the dividing line made by the corner of the room: On one side, you'd plunge into the past and on the other, you'd project yourself into the future. I started making a few drawings, and a friend came to visit me and I showed him my sketches. He was telling me about his new job and how he was using the new Microsoft Windows program on his computer with all these windows opening simultaneously. It clicked! I realized I could have multiple panels in the work, showing different times, in the same space. I worked on the story over the next few months, then I sent it to Spiegelman."

At the time, Spiegelman was co-editor of *RAW* magazine, an international, large-format

«Ich hatte an der Rutgers Bildhauerei studiert und war also mit den verschiedensten Werkzeugen und Techniken vertraut», schildert McGuire. Da die Computergrafik damals noch in den Kinderschuhen steckte, wurden häufig speziell angefertigte Requisiten verwendet. «Wenn es sich zum Beispiel um Werbung für eine Armbanduhr handelte, so bauten wir eine grossformatige Version, damit wir sie während des Drehs richtig beleuchten konnten. Wenn es um eine Mondlandschaft ging, dann schufen wir eine solche. Ein brennender Baum in der Wüste? Kein Problem. Ich habe mich sehr für den Film interessiert, und der Job bot mir die Möglichkeit, mich dem Medium zu nähern und es besser zu verstehen.»

Der Job war auch ein Türöffner. «Einmal habe ich an einem Werbespot gearbeitet, bei dem Animationen mit dreidimensionalen Hintergründen kombiniert wurden, die ich entworfen und gebaut hatte. Die Firma, die die Animation machte, sah nach mehr Spass aus, also überzeugte ich sie, mich einzustellen.» Sie produzierten auch Pee-wee Hermans Fernsehserie ‹Pee-wee's Playhouse› (Pee-wees Spielhaus) unter der künstlerischen Leitung von Gary Panter. «Es war eine wilde Zeit», fügt McGuire hinzu, «mit vielen Kunst- und Musikschaffenden, die am Projekt beteiligt waren.»

In der Animationsfirma arbeitete er mit einem Freiberufler zusammen, der gleichzeitig auch ein Zeichner war. «Ich bewunderte die Tatsache, dass er mehr Kontrolle über seine Zeit hatte. Ich war neidisch!», verrät McGuire. «Ich fragte ihn nach seinen Anfängen.» Danach «stellte ich ein Portfolio zusammen und begann, Aufträge von ‹The New York Times›, der ‹Village Voice› und schliesslich von ‹The New Yorker› zu bekommen».

Dieser stetige Strom von Illustrationsaufträgen ermöglichte es McGuire, das Animationsstudio zu verlassen und sich neuen Projekten zu widmen. In den späten 1980er-Jahren besuchte er eine Vorlesungsreihe von Art Spiegelman, der kurz darauf für seine Graphic Novel ‹Maus› den Pulitzer-Preis gewinnen sollte. «In einer seiner Vorlesungen sprach er [Spiegelman] über Comics als ‹narrative Diagramme›», berichtet McGuire. «Das Wort ‹Diagramm› fand bei mir Anklang.»

«Ich war gerade in eine neue Wohnung gezogen und dachte über die Person nach, die vor mir dort gewohnt hatte, sowie über die Person davor, und das brachte mich auf eine Idee, von der ich dachte, sie könnte interessant sein. Und zwar

The first concept sketch for Here / Die erste Konzeptskizze für ‹Hier›, pen on paper / Kugelschreiber auf Papier, 1988.

publication for avant-garde comics. "He called a few days after I sent the work and said he was interested in publishing it." His six-page story, Here, appeared in the magazine in 1989, in vol. 2, no. 1.

In 1990, McGuire's work entered a new phase with the release of his first toy, Puzzlehead, which he developed while working for the television production company. "Puzzlehead began with a doodle on graph paper while I was on the phone. I liked it enough to turn it into a prototype." He showed it to Steven Guarnaccia, now head of the illustration program at Parsons School of Design, in New York, who was working on a book about artists who make toys. A toy designer named Byron Glaser saw the prototype in his studio. "He liked it. He called me, and pretty soon, I was in Indonesia working with his manufacturing team."

Children's books came next. McGuire's first, The Orange Book, was published in 1992. "The idea came to me when I spotted an orange on the

wollte ich die Geschichte dieses Ortes in Form eines Bildschirms erzählen, der durch die Trennlinie in der Zimmerecke geteilt wird: Auf der einen Seite taucht man in die Vergangenheit ein, auf der anderen Seite projiziert man sich in die Zukunft. Ich begann, ein paar Zeichnungen anzufertigen, und zeigte meine Skizzen einem Freund, der zu Besuch kam. Er erzählte mir von seinem neuen Job, wie er das neue Microsoft-Windows-Programm auf seinem Computer benutzt und wie es all diese Fenster gleichzeitig öffnet. Da machte es klick! Mir wurde klar, dass ich im Werk mehrere Panels haben könnte, die verschiedene Zeiten im selben Raum zeigen. In den nächsten Monaten arbeitete ich an der Geschichte und schickte sie dann an Spiegelman.»

Art Spiegelman war damals Mitherausgeber des Magazins ‹RAW›, einer internationalen, grossformatigen Publikation für Avantgarde-Comics. «Ein paar Tage nachdem ich ihm die Arbeit geschickt hatte, rief er mich an und sagte, er sei an einer Veröffentlichung interessiert.» McGuires

Puzzlehead, prototype fabricated by / Prototyp hergestellt von Naef; wood, lacquer paint, silkscreen print / Holz, Lackfarbe, Siebdruck, 2007. Photo/Foto: Bill Orcutt.

subway tracks and thought, 'Oh that poor orange, what a tragic fate! What happened to all the other oranges?' I thought about it more as a metaphor for the path of life and individual destiny." Three more books would follow. *Night Becomes Day* (1994) is a meditation on how everything is connected; *What Goes Around Comes Around* (1995) explores the consequences of one's actions; and *What's Wrong with This Book?* (1997) is about perception and illusion. "These are some of my favorite subjects. I tried to present them in a way that speaks to kids."

McGuire's work in comics and children's books would give rise to a longtime collaboration with *The New Yorker*, which continues to this day. "Françoise Mouly, Art Spiegelman's wife and co-editor of *RAW*, had become the art director of *The New Yorker*," McGuire recalls. "One day, I went to visit Art and Françoise to show them my children's books and toys. Afterwards, Françoise called me and said 'I love what you're doing, you should really work for *The New Yorker*.'"

"The New Year was approaching and the magazine had to find a cover for the end-of-year double issue. I said, 'How about an image you can look at right side up or upside down?' She liked the idea. I made a few sketches, but nobody was convinced. Then I did another, which Françoise presented during an editorial meeting to Tina Brown, the editor-in-chief, but she found it too bizarre. Luckily, the sketch stayed on the desk and at the next meeting, just as Françoise was about to leave, Si Newhouse, the magazine's publisher and Tina Brown's boss, came

sechsseitige Geschichte ‹Here› (Hier) erschien 1989 in der Ausgabe 1 im Volume 2 des Magazins.

1990 trat McGuires Arbeit in eine neue Phase ein, als er sein erstes Spielzeug, ‹Puzzlehead› (Puzzlekopf), herausbrachte, das er während seiner Arbeit für die Fernsehproduktionsfirma entwickelt hatte. «‹Puzzlehead› begann mit einer Telefonkritzelei auf Millimeterpapier. Sie gefiel mir so gut, dass ich sie in einen Prototyp verwandelte.» Er zeigte ihn Steven Guarnaccia, dem heutigen Leiter des Studiengangs Illustration an der Parsons School of Design in New York, der gerade an einem Buch arbeitete über Kunstschaffende, die Spielsachen herstellen. Ein Spielzeugdesigner namens Byron Glaser sah den Prototyp in seinem Studio. «Er gefiel ihm. Er rief mich an, und schon bald darauf war ich in Indonesien und arbeitete mit seinem Produktionsteam zusammen.»

Als nächstes kamen Kinderbücher. McGuires erstes Buch, ‹The Orange Book› (Das Orangenbuch), wurde 1992 veröffentlicht. «Die Idee kam mir, als ich eine Orange auf den U-Bahn-Gleisen entdeckte und dachte: ‹Oh, diese arme Orange, was für ein tragisches Schicksal! Was ist nur mit all den anderen Orangen passiert?› Ich sah es eher als eine Metapher für den Lebensweg und das individuelle Schicksal.»

Drei weitere Bücher folgten: ‹Night Becomes Day› (Die Nacht wird zum Tag, 1994) ist eine Meditation darüber, wie alles zusammenhängt, ‹What Goes Around Comes Around› (Wie man in den Wald hineinruft, so schallt es heraus, 1995) erforscht die

City becomes building · And building becomes cloud

Night Becomes Day, published by / herausgegeben von Viking Penguin, 1992.

across it and thought it was a very good idea. To which Tina replied, 'Yes, that's our new cover!'" Since 1993, McGuire has produced 23 covers for *The New Yorker*, including 3 for its special issues. "It was important for me to work for this magazine, as so many of my heroes are associated with it."

He has also done countless spot illustrations for the magazine. These are the small graphics scattered throughout the articles. "They exist outside the text and tell a story, like little visual poems, a bit like haikus," McGuire explains. His spots are collected in *Sequential Drawings*, published by Pantheon in 2016.

In 1999, just a few years into his relationship with *The New Yorker*, McGuire's children's books would indirectly bring him back into the world of TV, when he was hired to do work for PBS, a public television network specializing in educational and cultural content. "They were starting a new division, PBS Kids. Knowing my children's books, they asked me to design the logo," as well as the interstitial animations that punctuated the programs. The logo remained in use for more than two decades.

By 2001, he had turned his attention back to books, this time for an older audience. First came *Popeye and Olive*, an edition of 200 silkscreen books published by Cornelius. A sequel, *P+O*, appeared in 2002. Both were an opportunity for McGuire to pay homage to the characters created by Segar, whom he is particularly fond of. "The books started with my decision to go on a meditation retreat at a Zen monastery. It was a silent weekend retreat, which included a class in Chinese calligraphy painting. The

Konsequenzen des eigenen Handelns und ‹What's Wrong with This Book?› (Was stimmt nicht mit diesem Buch?, 1997) handelt von Wahrnehmung und Illusion. «Das sind einige meiner Lieblingsthemen. Ich habe versucht, sie auf eine Weise zu präsentieren, die Kinder anspricht.»

McGuires Arbeit an Comics und Kinderbüchern führte zu einer langjährigen Zusammenarbeit mit ‹The New Yorker›, die bis heute andauert. «Françoise Mouly, Art Spiegelmans Frau und Mitherausgeberin von ‹RAW›, war inzwischen künstlerische Leiterin bei ‹The New Yorker›», erinnert sich McGuire. «Eines Tages besuchte ich Art und Françoise, um ihnen meine Kinderbücher und Spielzeuge zu zeigen. Danach rief mich Françoise an und sagte: ‹Mir gefällt, was du machst, du solltest wirklich für ‹The New Yorker› arbeiten.›»

«Das neue Jahr stand vor der Tür und das Magazin musste ein Cover für die Doppelausgabe zum Jahresende finden. Also schlug ich vor: ‹Wie wäre es mit einem Bild, das man sowohl richtig herum als auch auf dem Kopf stehend betrachten kann?› Die Idee gefiel ihr. Ich machte ein paar Skizzen, aber niemand war überzeugt. Ich zeichnete eine weitere, die Françoise in einer Redaktionssitzung der Chefredakteurin Tina Brown zeigte, aber sie fand sie zu bizarr. Glücklicherweise blieb die Skizze auf dem Schreibtisch liegen. Bei der nächsten Sitzung, als Françoise gerade gehen wollte, entdeckte sie dort Si Newhouse, der Verleger des Magazins und Tina Browns Chef. Und er hielt die Skizze für eine sehr gute Idee. Daraufhin antwortete Tina: ‹Ja, das ist unser neues Cover!› Seit 1993 hat McGuire 23 Cover für ‹The New Yorker› gestaltet, darunter für

class required painting the same character over and over again, like repeating a mantra, a practice of meditation through repeated painting. Back home, I continued the exercise and one day, one of the shapes suggested the silhouette of the Popeye character. I decided to riff on Popeye's and Olive's silhouettes and created a series of variations. In the books, Popeye and Olive meet, and from that point on, their shapes merge and compose a language of relationship." He calls it "an abstract love story." (In 2023, *Popeye and Olive* was reissued by Fotokino, along with a series of woodblock prints, produced by The Arm in Brooklyn.)

He had also begun to think about reworking *Here*, the comic published in 1989 in *RAW*. In 2000, the Swiss magazine *Strapazin* had published McGuire's drei seiner Sonderausgaben. «Es war wichtig für mich, für dieses Magazin zu arbeiten, da so viele meiner Helden mit ihm verbunden sind.»

Er hat für das Magazin auch unzählige Spot-Illustrationen gezeichnet, also die kleinen Grafiken, die in den Artikeln verstreut sind. «Sie existieren ausserhalb des Textes und erzählen eine Geschichte, wie kleine visuelle Gedichte, so ein bisschen wie Haikus», erläutert McGuire. Seine Spot-Illustrationen sind in ‹Sequential Drawings› (Fortlaufende Zeichnungen) gesammelt, das 2016 bei Pantheon erschienen ist.

Im Jahr 1999, nur wenige Jahre nach Beginn seiner Zusammenarbeit mit ‹The New Yorker›, brachten ihn seine Kinderbücher auf indirektem Weg zurück

Time Warp, cover for / Titelseite für The New Yorker, Nov. 2014.

Subway, spot series / Spot-Serie, The New Yorker, 2011.

remixed color version of the comic, and the idea of turning the work into a full-fledged graphic novel started to take shape. However, the project had to be put on hold in 2002, when McGuire was presented with the opportunity to experiment in a new form, working with the French production company Prima Linea on *Loulou et autres loups*. The omnibus feature, written by Grégoire Solotareff and Jean-Luc Fromental, included four short films. One was *Micro Loup*, designed and directed by McGuire.

"I had just produced *ctrl*, a comic strip for an issue of *McSweeney's Quarterly* guest-edited by Chris Ware. It was a short story presented from a bird's-eye view, and I'd done a *New Yorker* cover based on the same principle. I suggested that they use this same point of view for *Micro Loup*. At first, [the Prima Linea team] didn't know what to make of it, but I explained that with sound, everything would become clear. In the end, they were very happy, so much so that they immediately talked to me about another project, *Peur(s) du noir (Fear(s) of the Dark)*."

For this project, which premiered in 2007 at the Rome Film Fest, he was one of six illustrators chosen to create and direct the short films that make up the program. (The film's other directors include Lorenzo Mattoti, Blutch, and Charles Burns.) Each film is made exclusively in black and white, a constraint that led McGuire to develop an original graphic solution that sets his work apart.

in die Welt des Fernsehens, als er von PBS, einem öffentlichen Fernsehsender mit Fokus auf pädagogische und kulturelle Inhalte, für einen Job eingestellt wurde. «Sie waren dabei, eine neue Abteilung – PBS Kids – zu gründen. Da sie meine Kinderbücher kannten, baten sie mich, das Logo zu entwerfen.» Weiter gestaltete McGuire die Kurzanimationen zwischen den Programmen. Das Logo blieb über zwei Jahrzehnte in Gebrauch.

Im Jahr 2001 wandte er sich wieder den Büchern zu, diesmal für ein älteres Publikum. Zuerst erschien ‹Popeye and Olive› (Popeye und Olive), eine Auflage von 200 Siebdruckbüchern, die von Cornelius veröffentlicht wurden. Eine Fortsetzung, ‹P+O›, erschien im Jahr 2002. Beide waren für McGuire eine Gelegenheit, die Figuren des von ihm sehr geschätzten Segars zu würdigen. «Die Bücher begannen mit meiner Entscheidung, an einem Meditations-Retreat in einem Zen-Kloster teilzunehmen. Es war ein Schweigewochenende, zu dem auch ein Kurs in chinesischer Kalligraphie gehörte. Im Kurs ging es darum, immer wieder dasselbe Zeichen zu malen, wie das Wiederholen eines Mantras, also eine Meditationspraxis durch wiederholtes Malen. Zu Hause setzte ich die Übung fort, und eines Tages erinnerte mich eine der Formen an den Umriss der Popeye-Figur. Ich beschloss, mit den Silhouetten von Popeye und Olive zu spielen und schuf eine Reihe von Variationen. In den Büchern treffen sich Popeye und Olive, und von diesem Zeitpunkt an verschmelzen ihre Formen und bilden eine Sprache der Beziehung.» McGuire nennt es «eine abstrakte Liebesgeschichte». (2023 wurde ‹Popeye and Olive› von Fotokino neu aufgelegt, zusammen mit einer Serie von Holzschnitten, gedruckt von The Arm in Brooklyn.)

Er dachte auch darüber nach, seinen 1989 in ‹RAW› erschienenen Comic ‹Here› zu überarbeiten. Im Jahr 2000 veröffentlichte das Schweizer Magazin ‹Strapazin› McGuires neu abgemischte Farbversion des Comics, und die Idee, das Werk in eine vollwertige Graphic Novel zu verwandeln, nahm Gestalt an. Das Projekt musste jedoch 2002 vorerst auf Eis gelegt werden, als sich McGuire mit der Arbeit an ‹Loulou et autres loups› der französischen Produktionsfirma Prima Linea die Gelegenheit bot, mit einer neuen Form zu experimentieren. Der von Grégoire Solotareff und Jean-Luc Fromental geschriebene Episodenfilm umfasste vier Kurzfilme. Einer davon war ‹Micro Loup›, bei dem McGuire die Gestaltung und Regie übernahm.

P+O, published by / herausgegeben von Cornelius, France/Frankreich, 2001.

"I used my own anxieties, like claustrophobia, to conceive the story. But at the very beginning of work on the film, while researching my way through this new project, I came across the graphic work of Félix Valloton, a Swiss artist from the turn of the last century who, among other graphic experiments, used black on black—characters dressed in black, for example, against a black background. When I discovered this, I said to myself that it was my gateway to push the idea even further. This project took me several years to complete. But I loved this new job as director." In 2008, he presented *Peur(s) du noir* (*Fear(s) of the Dark*) at the Sundance Film Festival.

A year later, McGuire was awarded a grant from the New York Public Library to undertake research that enabled him to devote himself to the expanded version of *Here*, and, in 2014, the book was published in the United States by Pantheon. "I wanted the book to relate to the first version,

«Ich hatte gerade ‹ctrl› produziert, einen Comicstrip für eine Ausgabe von ‹McSweeney's Quarterly›, für die Chris Ware Gastherausgeber war. Es handelte sich dabei um eine Kurzgeschichte aus der Vogelperspektive. Ich hatte nach demselben Prinzip ein Cover für ‹The New Yorker› gemacht und schlug vor, diesen gleichen Blickwinkel für ‹Micro Loup› zu verwenden. Zuerst wussten sie [das Prima-Linea-Team] nicht, was sie davon halten sollten, aber ich erklärte ihnen, dass mit Ton alles klar werden würde. Am Ende waren sie sehr zufrieden, so sehr sogar, dass sie mit mir gleich über ein weiteres Projekt sprachen: ‹Peur(s) du noir› (Angstgefühl(e) vor der Dunkelheit).»

McGuire war einer der sechs Illustrationsschaffenden, die für die Gestaltung und Regie der Kurzfilme dieses 2007 auf der Festa del Cinema di Roma uraufgeführten Projekts ausgewählt wurden. (Zu den anderen Regisseuren des Films gehören Lorenzo Mattoti, Blutch und

Here/‹Hier›, end pages / Endblätter, published by / herausgegeben von Pantheon, 2014.

without imitating its style. I couldn't just add pages to something I'd done 25 years ago," McGuire says. The narrative and graphic principles would remain the same, with the story told from a single point of view, but the anonymous living room would now be based on the one in McGuire's family home. "I knew I could go deeper. I wanted something more personal, more emotional."

In the new version, the entire room is seen across a two-page spread, with the corner of the room at the center. "When you open the book, you're entering the room and the book becomes a kind of sculptural object." A succession of temporal fragments enliven each page, taking the reader on a journey through billions of years, from the appearance of life on Earth to the distant future. This fresco, in which time is the main protagonist, presents a continuous shuffle of memories and projections with a simultaneity akin to the way we think: rarely in the present, more often than not anticipating the future or rethinking past moments.

Here quickly became a major work in the history of comics. In 2016, the French version, *Ici*, won the Fauve d'or, France's top award for graphic novels. In 2022, it was announced that a film adaptation

Charles Burns). Jeder Kurzfilm ist ausschliesslich in Schwarzweiss gedreht – eine Vorgabe, die McGuire zum Entwickeln einer originellen grafischen Lösung veranlasste, die seine Arbeit von den anderen unterscheidet.

«Ich nutzte meine eigenen Ängste, wie etwa Klaustrophobie, um mir die Geschichte auszudenken. Gleich zu Beginn der Arbeit am Film, während meiner Recherchen zu diesem neuen Projekt, stiess ich jedoch auf das grafische Werk von Félix Vallotton, einem Schweizer Künstler der Wende vom 19. ins 20. Jahrhundert, der – neben anderen grafischen Experimenten – Schwarz auf Schwarz benutzte, wie beispielsweise schwarz gekleidete Figuren vor einem schwarzen Hintergrund. Diese Entdeckung, so sagte ich mir, war mein Ausgangspunkt, von dem aus ich meine Idee weiterentwickeln konnte. Ich brauchte mehrere Jahre, um dieses Projekt zu realisieren. Aber ich liebte diese neue Aufgabe als Regisseur.» Im Jahr 2008 präsentierte er ‹Peur(s) du noir› (Angstgefühl(e) vor der Dunkelheit) auf dem Sundance Film Festival.

Ein Jahr später erhielt McGuire ein Forschungsstipendium der New York Public Library,

of *Here* would be directed by Robert Zemeckis, starring Tom Hanks and Robin Wright—the trio behind the global hit *Forrest Gump*. It is scheduled to be released in 2024.

McGuire continues to see each new project as an artistic playground for developing new ideas. A case in point is the installation he conceived in 2018 for The Aldrich Contemporary Art Museum, in Ridgefield, Connecticut. In *The Way There and Back*, he presented 62 sculptures of shoes. The objects verged on pure abstraction and evoked the cacophony of the street. Made of wood, plaster, or resin, and named after people who were meaningful to him, the shoes are part of his personal conversation with the culture and history of New York City. "One day, I sculpted a shoe and called it Lou, because it reminded me of a shoe Lou Reed might have worn. Then I started making other shoes. I felt more like a shoemaker than a sculptor. I liked to go to the studio knowing what I had to do, even if I sometimes thought it was a stupid idea. In the evening, I'd leave the studio full of doubts, and the next day, I'd arrive and the shapes that were born would make me happy. That was enough to keep me going."

Here/‹Hier›, book cover / Buchumschlag, published by / herausgegeben von Pantheon, 2014.

das ihm ermöglichte, sich der erweiterten Fassung von ‹Here› zu widmen. 2014 erschien das Buch dann in den USA bei Pantheon. «Ich wollte, dass sich das Buch auf die erste Fassung bezieht, ohne deren Stil zu imitieren. Ich konnte nicht einfach Seiten zu etwas hinzufügen, das ich vor 25 Jahren gemacht hatte», erörtert McGuire. Während die erzählerischen und grafischen Prinzipien gleich bleiben und die Geschichte weiterhin aus einer einzigen Perspektive erzählt wird, basiert das anonyme Wohnzimmer nun auf demjenigen in McGuires Elternhaus. «Ich wusste, dass ich tiefer gehen konnte. Ich wollte etwas Persönlicheres, Emotionaleres.»

In der neuen Fassung ist das gesamte Zimmer auf einer Doppelseite zu sehen, wobei die Ecke des Zimmers im Mittelpunkt steht. «Wenn man das Buch aufschlägt, betritt man den Raum, und das Buch wird zu einer Art skulpturalem Objekt.» Eine Abfolge von Zeitfragmenten belebt jede Seite und nimmt den Leser mit auf eine Reise durch Milliarden von Jahren, von der Entstehung des Lebens auf der Erde bis hin in die ferne Zukunft. Dieses Fresko, in dem die Zeit der Hauptdarsteller ist, zeigt ein ständiges Durcheinander von Erinnerungen und Projektionen mit einer Gleichzeitigkeit, die der Art und Weise ähnelt, wie wir denken: selten in der Gegenwart, meistens in Erwartung der Zukunft oder im Nachdenken über vergangene Momente.

‹Here› wurde schnell zu einem wichtigen Werk in der Geschichte des Comics. Die französische Version, ‹Ici›, wurde 2016 mit dem Fauve d'or ausgezeichnet, Frankreichs wichtigstem Preis für Graphic Novels. Für 2022 wurde eine Verfilmung von ‹Here› unter der Regie von Robert Zemeckis angekündigt, mit Tom Hanks und Robin Wright in den Hauptrollen – dem Trio hinter dem Welterfolg ‹Forrest Gump›. Der Film soll 2024 in die Kinos kommen.

McGuire betrachtet weiterhin jedes neue Projekt als künstlerische Spielwiese für die Entwicklung neuer Ideen. Ein Beispiel dafür ist die Installation, die er 2018 für das Aldrich Contemporary Art Museum in Ridgefield, Connecticut, konzipiert hat. In ‹The Way There and Back› (Der Weg hin und zurück) präsentierte er 62 Schuh-Skulpturen. Die Objekte grenzen an reine Abstraktion und erinnern an die Kakophonie der Strasse. Die aus Holz, Gips oder Harz gefertigten und nach ihm wichtigen Menschen benannten Schuhe sind Teil seiner persönlichen Auseinandersetzung mit der Kultur

Here/‹Hier›, film clapper / Filmklappe, 2023.

The Aldrich Museum also invited him to create a graphic suite to be included in the show's catalog. "Staying with the theme of 'small objects', I thought about all the things I touch in a day that I don't usually pay much attention to," McGuire explains. In *My Things*, he examines in detail the everyday gestures and simple interactions we have with the objects that surround us.

McGuire's attention to our most immediate environment is echoed in *Listen*, published by Fotokino on the occasion of his *Sound & Vision* exhibition in Marseille, in 2021. In this book, he puts his ear to the ground and stages a narrative made of sound. "There are 11 windows in my house, which allows me to capture the sounds coming from all sides," McGuire explains of his home in New York's Hudson Valley, north of New York City, where he moved in 2020 during the Covid lockdown. "That's where *Listen* comes from. Having lived in the city for so long, you become hypersensitive to all the sounds of the countryside; it's as if they've been amplified. That's the starting point for this book, but there's also the idea of graphically codifying sounds, a subject that has always interested me."

The *Listen* book also sparked two new projects. The first is a series of diagrammatic sound drawings. "I started drawing the diagrams as an exercise with no clear idea of where I was going with them. I set up some rules that I would follow and they started

und Geschichte von New York City. «Eines Tages gestaltete ich einen Schuh und nannte ihn Lou, weil er mich an einen Schuh erinnerte, den Lou Reed getragen haben könnte. Dann begann ich, weitere Schuhe herzustellen. Ich fühlte mich eher wie ein Schuhmacher als ein Bildhauer. Ich ging gern ins Atelier und wusste, was ich zu tun hatte, auch wenn ich es manchmal für eine dumme Idee hielt. Abends verliess ich das Atelier jeweils voller Zweifel, um am nächsten Tag wiederzukommen und mich über die entstandenen Formen zu freuen. Das reichte für mich zum Weitermachen.»

Das Aldrich Museum lud ihn weiter ein, eine grafische Folge zu entwerfen, die im Ausstellungskatalog aufgenommen werden sollte. «Um beim Thema ‹kleine Objekte› zu bleiben, habe ich über all die Dinge nachgedacht, mit denen ich täglich in Berührung komme und denen ich normalerweise nicht viel Aufmerksamkeit schenke», erläutert McGuire. In ‹My Things› (Meine Dinge) untersucht er im Detail die alltäglichen Gesten und einfachen Interaktionen, die wir mit den uns umgebenden Gegenständen haben.

McGuires Aufmerksamkeit für unsere unmittelbare Umgebung findet ihren Widerhall in ‹Listen› (Zuhören), das anlässlich seiner Ausstellung ‹Sound & Vision› (Ton & Bild) in Marseille 2021 von Fotokino veröffentlicht wurde. In diesem Buch legt er sein Ohr auf den Boden und inszeniert eine Erzählung aus Klang. «In meinem Haus gibt es elf Fenster, die es mir ermöglichen, die Geräusche von allen Seiten einzufangen», erklärt McGuire über sein nördlich von New York City, im Hudson Valley im US-Bundesstaat New York gelegene Haus, wohin er 2020 während des Covid-Lockdowns zog. «Das ist der Ursprung von ‹Listen›. Wenn man so lange in der Stadt gelebt hat, wird man überempfindlich für alle Geräusche auf dem Land – es ist, als ob sie verstärkt worden wären. Das ist der Ausgangspunkt für dieses Buch, aber auch die Idee, Geräusche grafisch zu verschlüsseln – ein Thema, das mich schon immer interessiert hat.»

Das ‹Listen›-Buch gab auch den Anstoss zu zwei neuen Projekten. Das erste ist eine Reihe von schematischen Klang-Zeichnungen. «Ich begann mit dem Zeichnen der Diagramme als Übung, ohne eine klare Vorstellung davon zu haben, was ich damit erreichen wollte. Ich stellte einige Regeln auf, die ich befolgen würde, und das Zeichnen erledigte sich dann praktisch von selbst. Die

to practically draw themselves. The structure and the words work together like a musical score." McGuire's other new project is an experimental graphic novel about the appreciation of sound. "The restraints are the exact opposite of *Here*. Instead of focusing on one location over all of time, this book takes place everywhere in the known universe, and unfolds over the course of just one minute."

Today, his work has gained international recognition and is present in the permanent collections of the Museum of Modern Art, the Metropolitan Museum of Art, the Morgan Library and Museum, and the Cooper Hewitt Smithsonian Design Museum. Nonetheless, McGuire continues to explore, experiment, and research, without worrying about the boundaries between genres but, on the contrary, with a desire for fusion, between sound and image in particular. *Then and There, Here and Now* reveals the diversity and richness of his output, tracing the extraordinary career of an unclassifiable artist.

Vincent Tuset-Anrès
•
The interview fragments with Richard McGuire collected here are the result of the ongoing dialog we've been having since 2020, when we were preparing the *Sound & Vision* exhibition at Studio Fotokino, and which we were able to continue during the conception of this book.

Struktur und die Worte wirken zusammen wie eine Partitur.» Das andere neue Projekt von McGuire ist eine experimentelle Graphic Novel über die Wertschätzung von Klang. «Die Einschränkungen sind das genaue Gegenteil von ‹Here›. Anstatt sich auf einen Ort in allen Zeiten zu konzentrieren, spielt dieses Buch überall im bekannten Universum und entfaltet sich im Laufe von nur einer Minute.»

Heute hat sein Werk internationale Anerkennung gefunden und ist in den ständigen Sammlungen des Museum of Modern Art, des Metropolitan Museum of Art, der Morgan Library and Museum sowie des Cooper Hewitt Smithsonian Design Museum vertreten. Nichtsdestotrotz erkundet, experimentiert und forscht McGuire weiter, ohne sich um die Grenzen zwischen den Genres zu kümmern, sondern ganz im Gegenteil mit dem Wunsch nach Verschmelzung, insbesondere zwischen Ton und Bild. ‹Then and There, Here and Now› zeigt die Vielfalt und den Reichtum seines Schaffens und zeichnet die aussergewöhnliche Karriere eines nicht klassifizierbaren Künstlers nach.

Vincent Tuset-Anrès
•
Die hier versammelten Interviewfragmente mit Richard McGuire sind das Ergebnis eines Dialogs, den wir seit 2020, als wir die Ausstellung ‹Sound & Vision› im Studio Fotokino vorbereiteten, kontinuierlich führen und den wir während der Konzeption dieses Buches fortsetzen konnten.

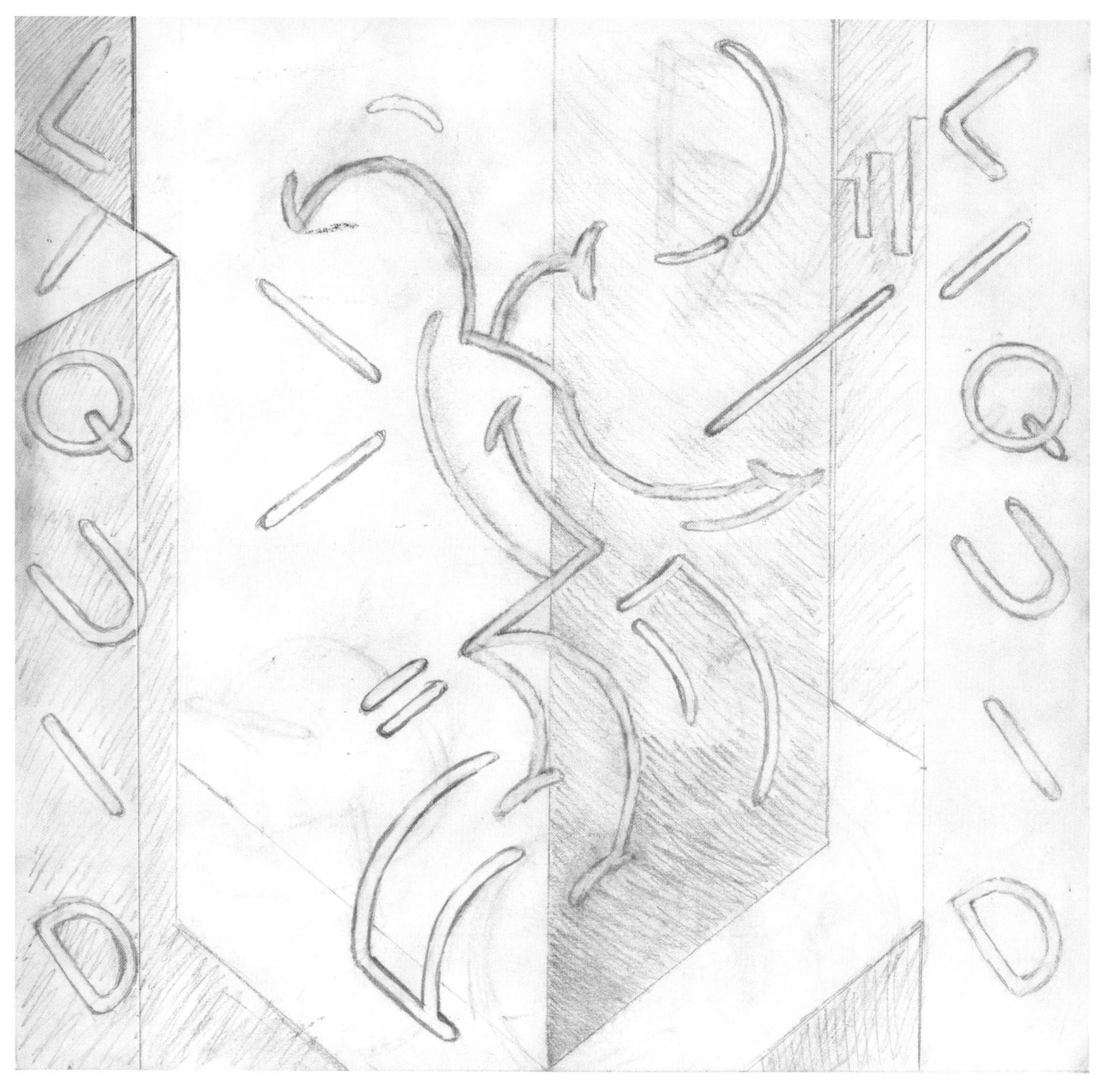

1981

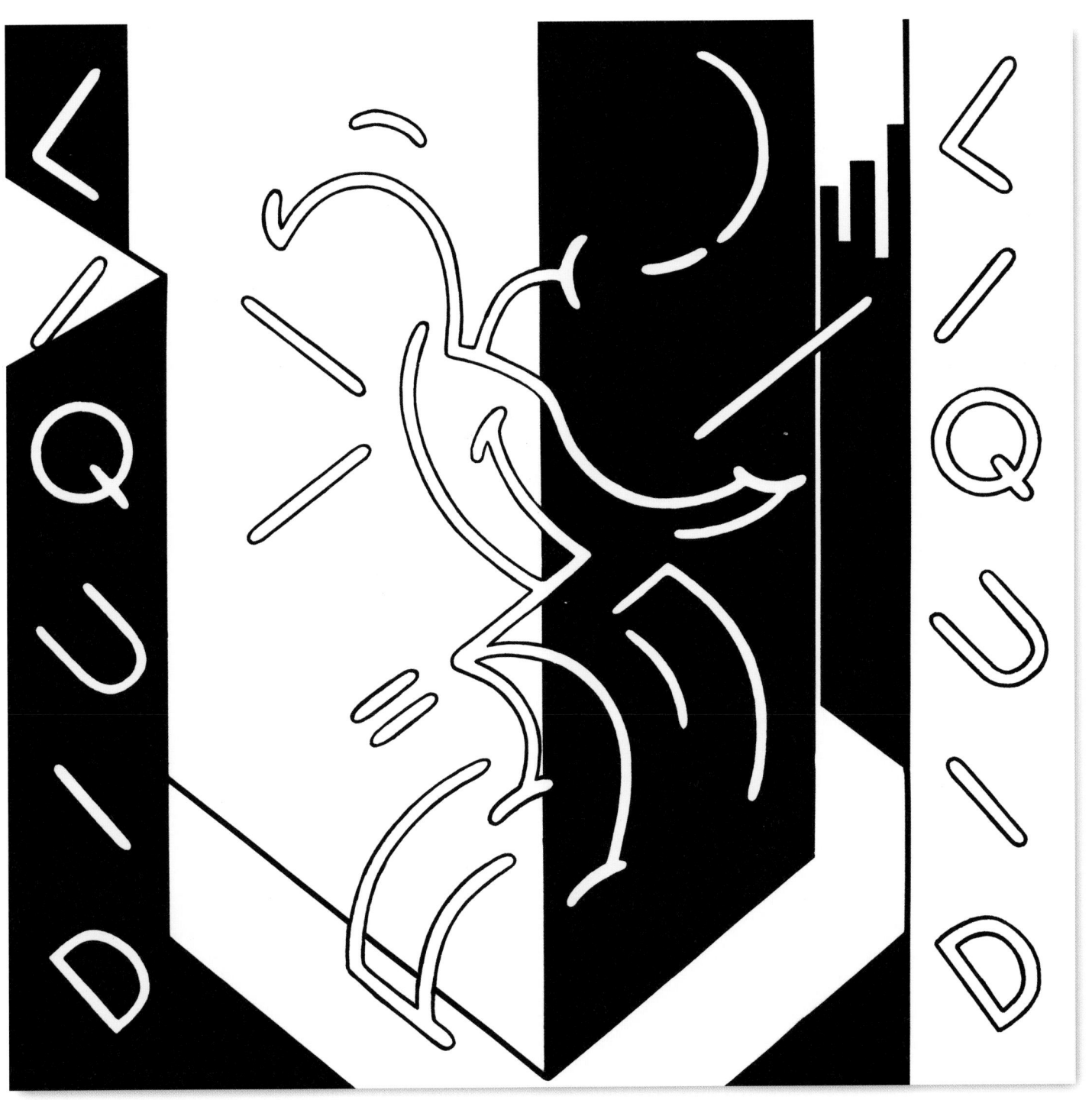

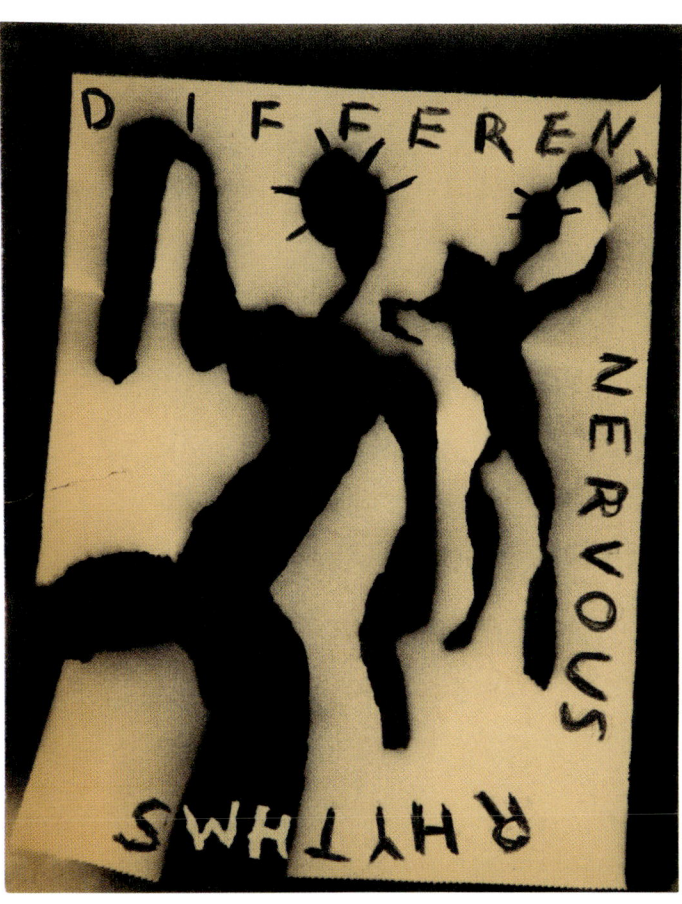

1979, 1980, 1981

1979

32

1980

2019

2023

2023

2015

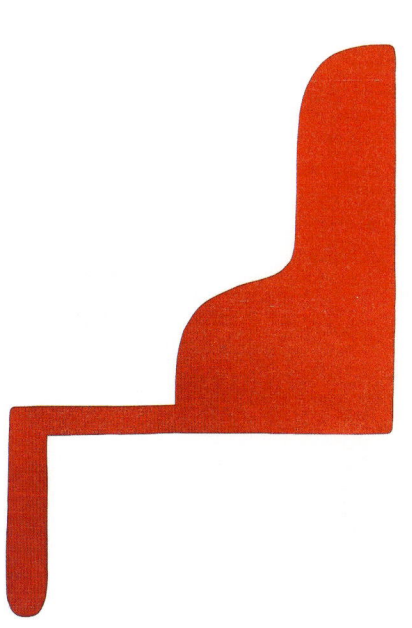

2023

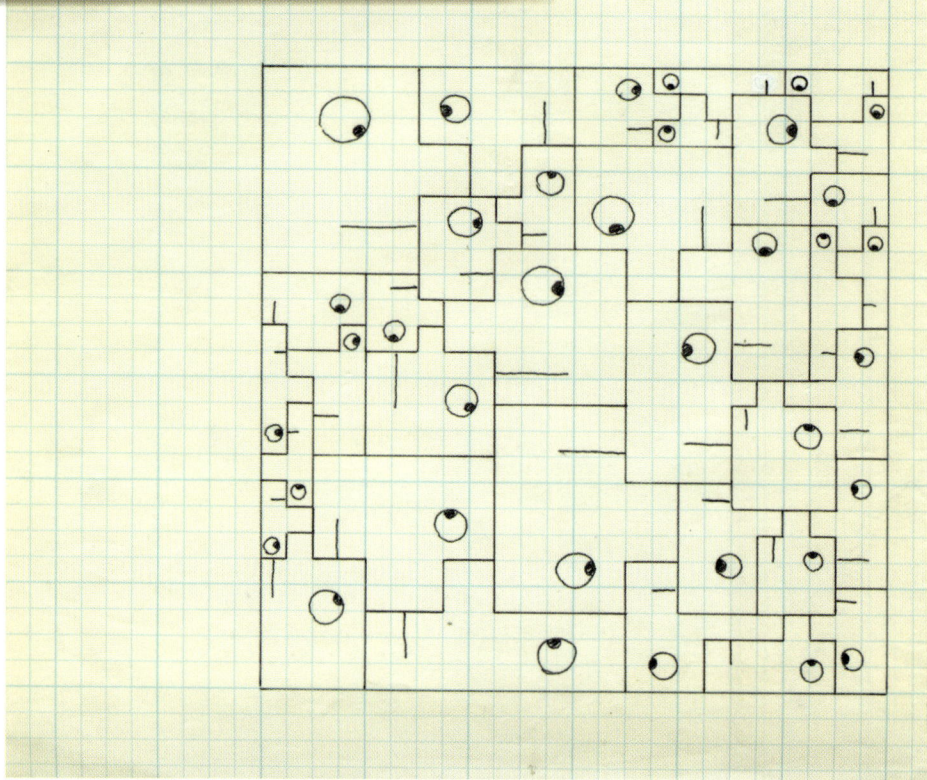

40

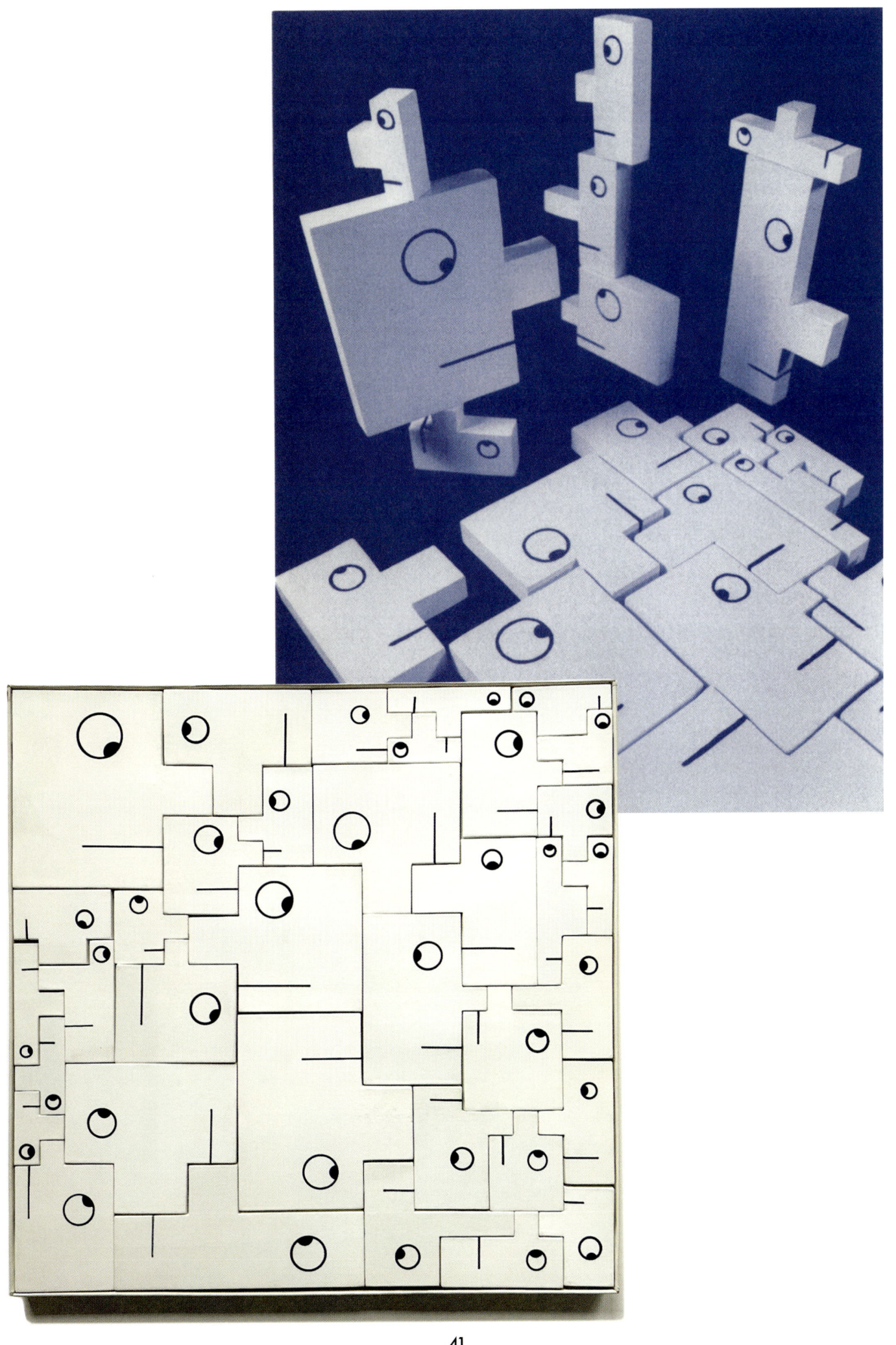

1990

ARCHER

ROPER

PASSENGER

WHISTLER

DRUMMER

STRANGER

FORTUNE-TELLER

BYSTANDER

DANCER

YODELER

FIRE-EATER

JOKER

ROBBER

GEEZER

SNEAKER

GHOSTWRITER

BOXER

RIVETER

WAITER

THINKER

1991 – 2016

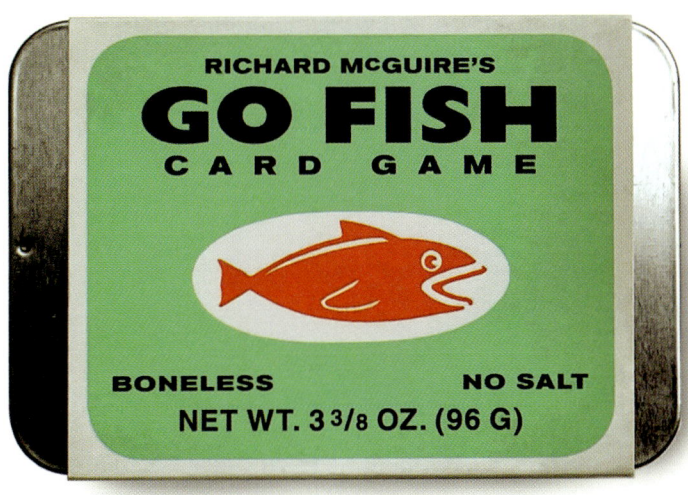

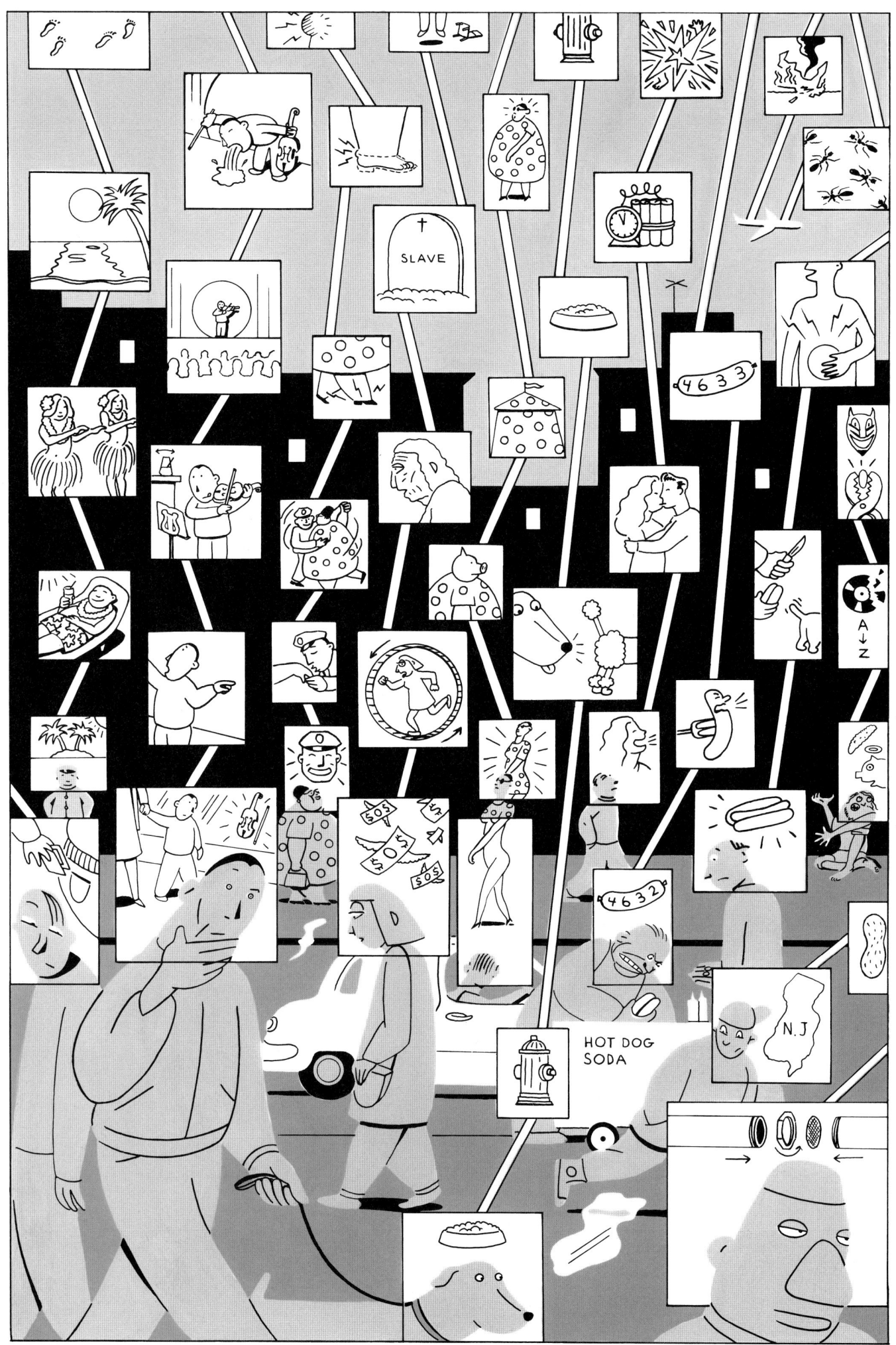

1994

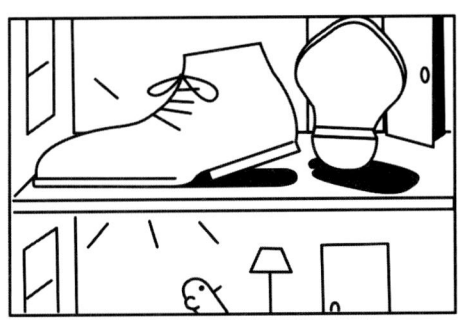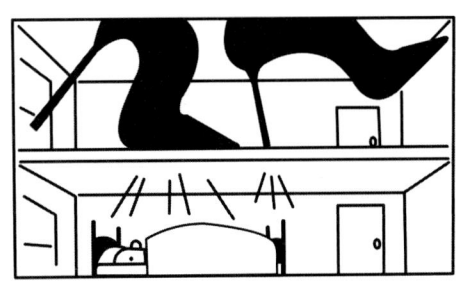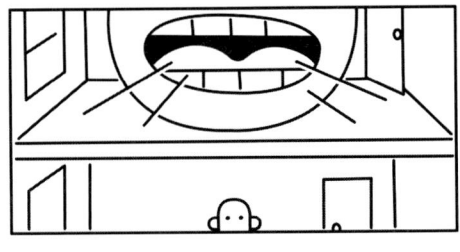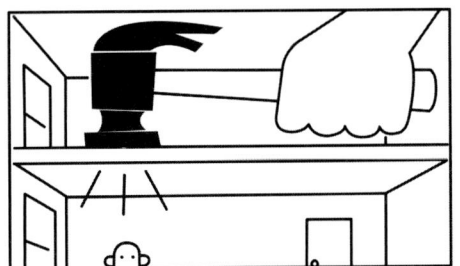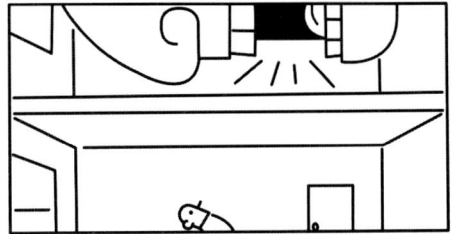

1978

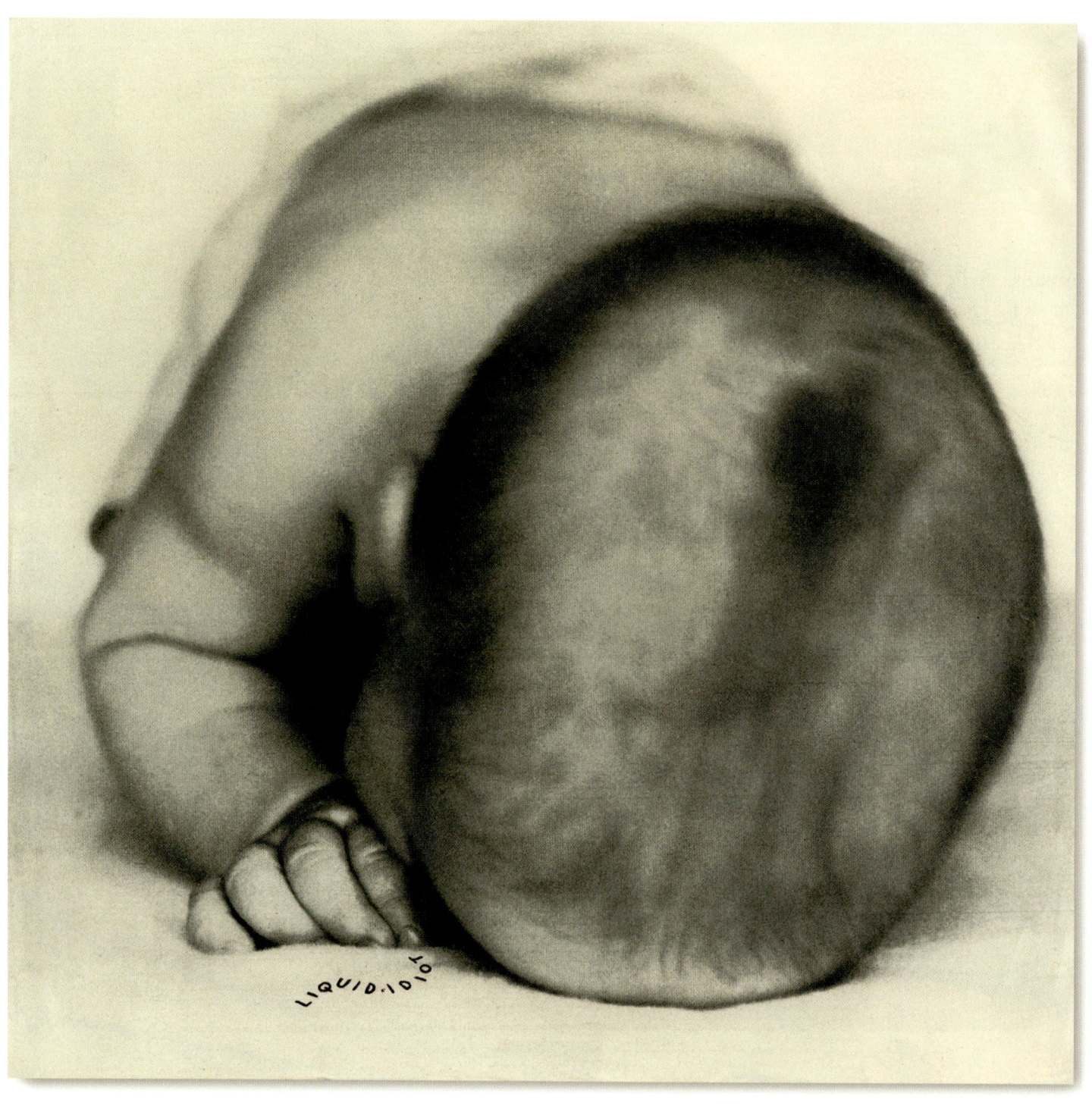

2000

STRAPAZIN

Das Comic Magazin, Nr. 88, September 2007
Euro 6.–, sFr. 10.–

2005

PEUR [S]
DU NOIR

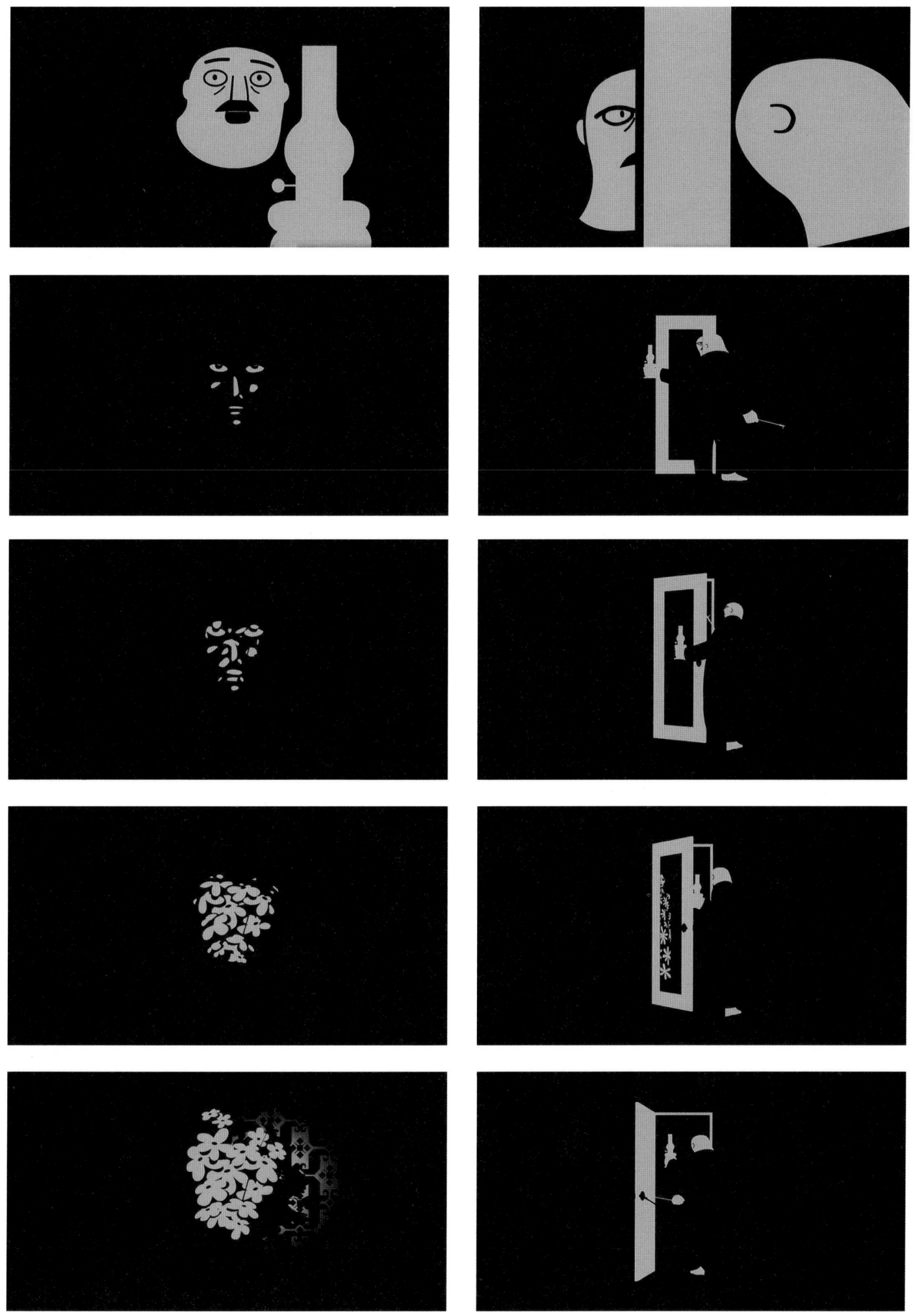

1994

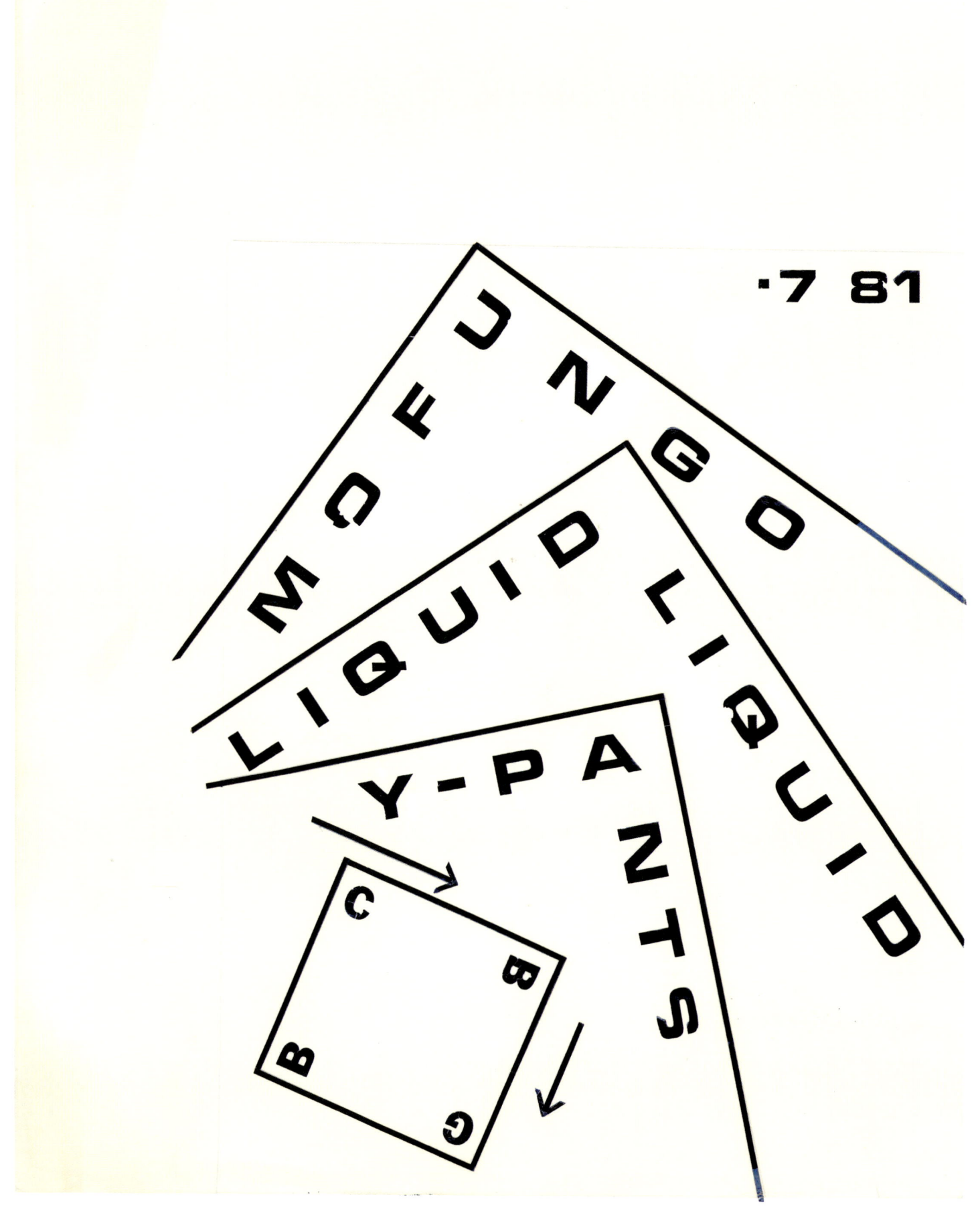

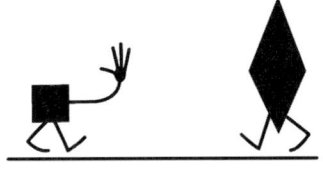

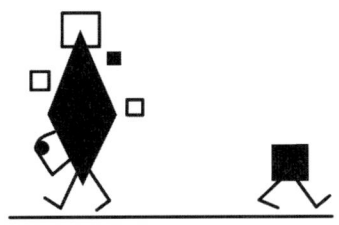

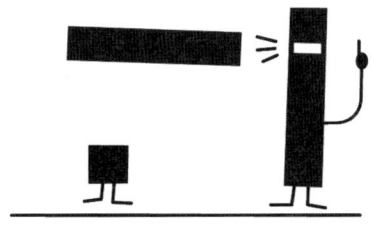
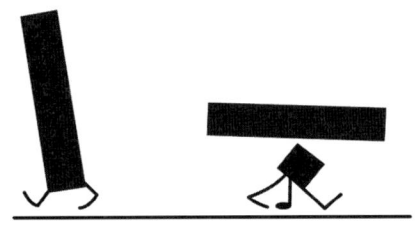

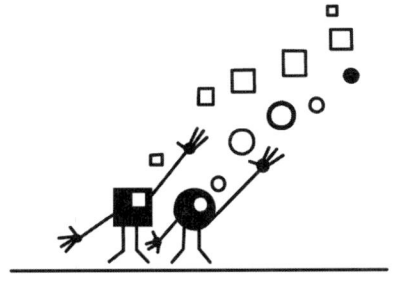

1996

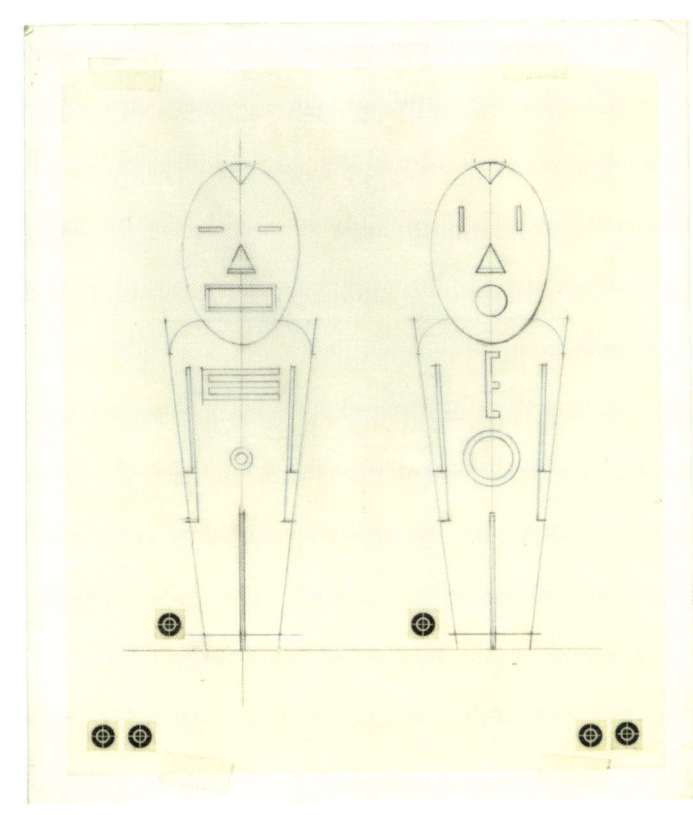

1992

One was sent to a sick friend.

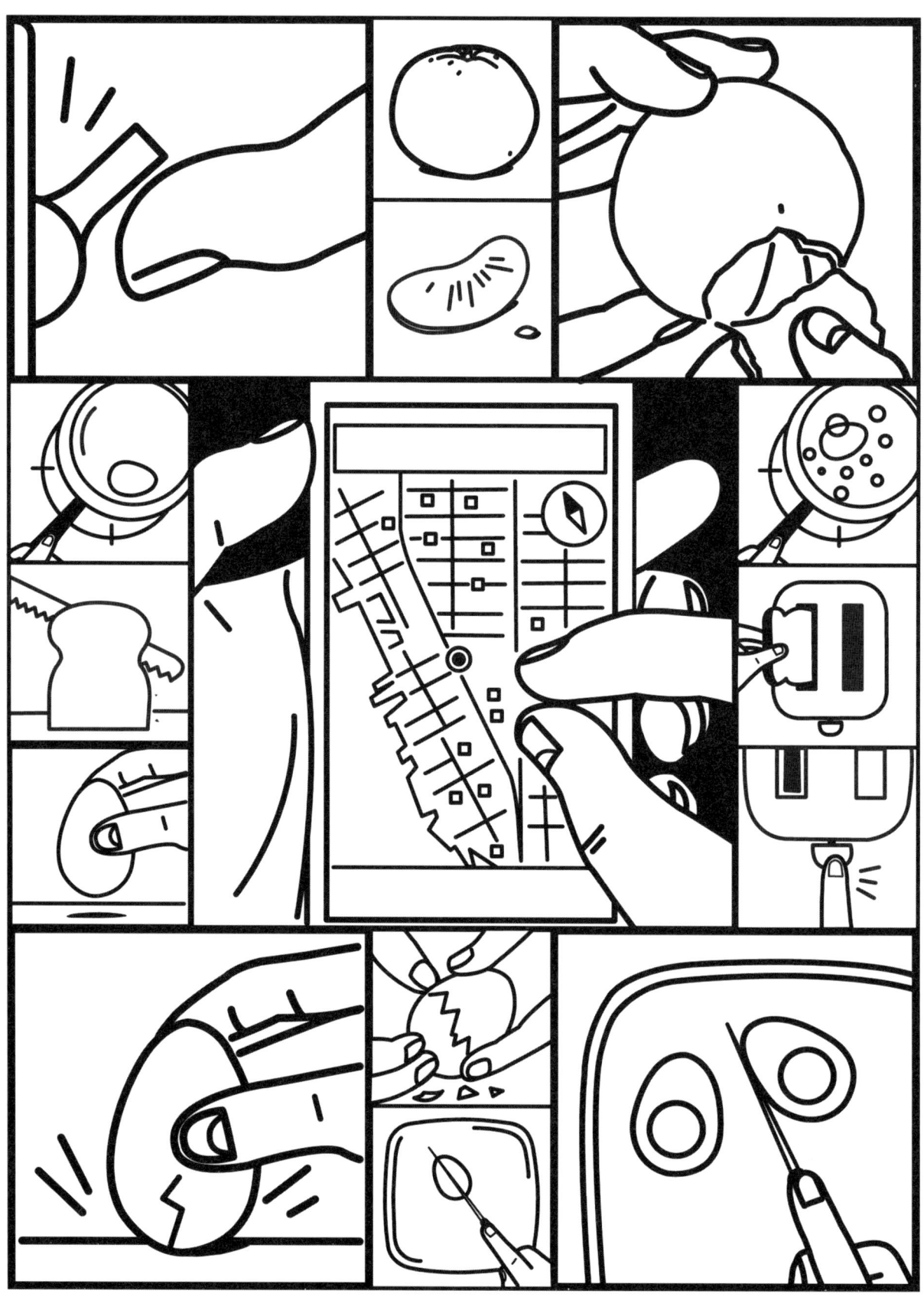

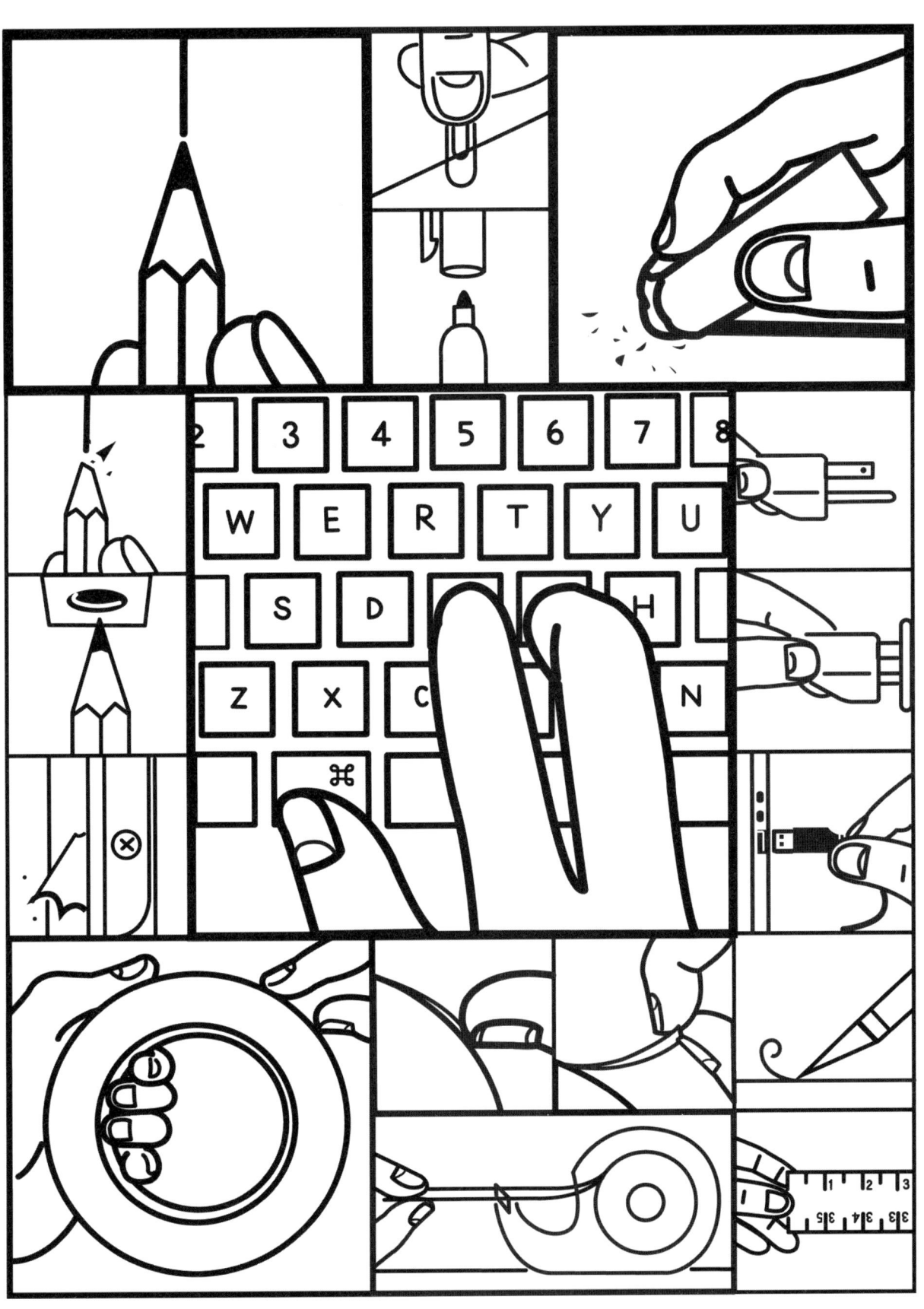

2002

2024

Wie wäre es, fragt sich der Zeichner **Richard McGuire**, wenn alles, was je geschah, in einem einzigen Augenblick geschähe?

2016

„Zeit ist eine Illusion", schrieb Albert Einstein einmal in einem Brief an seine Schwester. Zeitmesser wie Uhren und Kalender halten uns auf Kurs in einer linearen Vorwärtsbewegung, aber in unseren Köpfen sind wir Zeitreisende. Ein Geruch bringt uns zurück in unsere Kindheit, eine Sekunde später erinnern wir uns an einen Termin und rasen wieder ins Heute. Wir sind immer wieder in Berührung mit unserer Gegenwart, aber halten selten inne, um den Augenblick, in dem wir uns befinden, wirklich auszukosten. Der bekannte italienische Quantenphysiker Carlo Rovelli glaubt, der Ablauf der Zeit hänge mit Temperaturschwankungen zusammen, selbst wenn diese nicht wahrnehmbar sind. Ich warte gerade darauf, dass das Wasser kocht, später wird der Tee die Hitze wieder abgeben. Ich habe mir oft vorgestellt, dass alle Zeit im selben Moment existiert, dass alles, was je geschah und je geschehen wird, im selben Moment geschieht. Ich stelle mir all diese warmen Menschen vor, wie sie den Staub aufwirbeln in einem einzigen Forever Now. **RICHARD MCGUIRE**

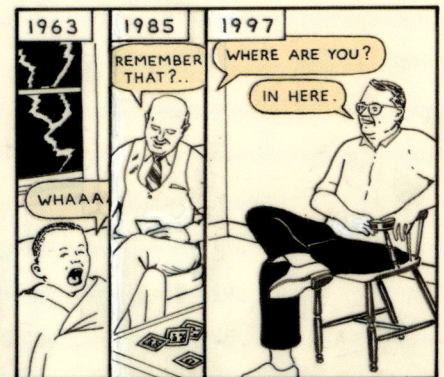

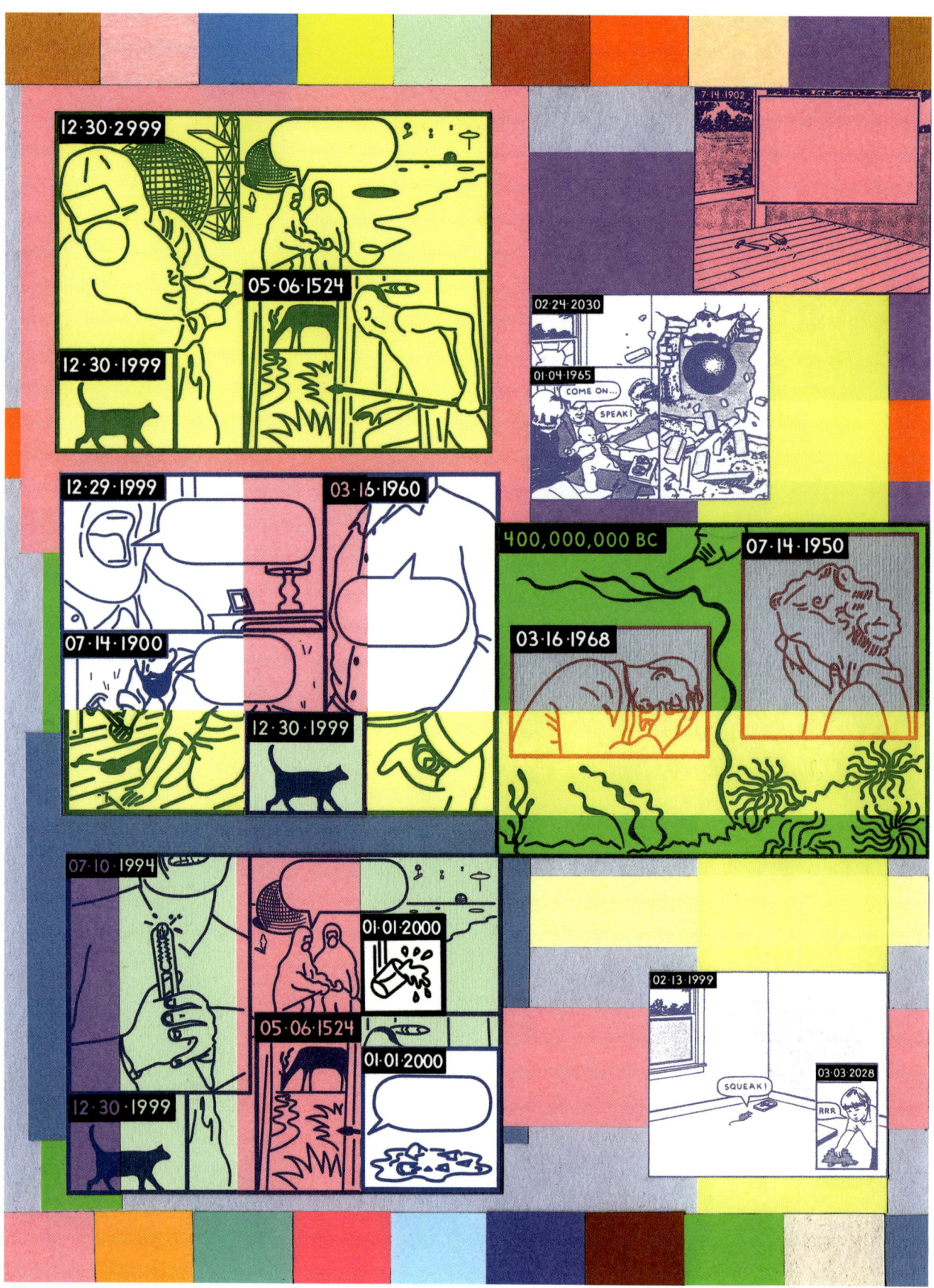

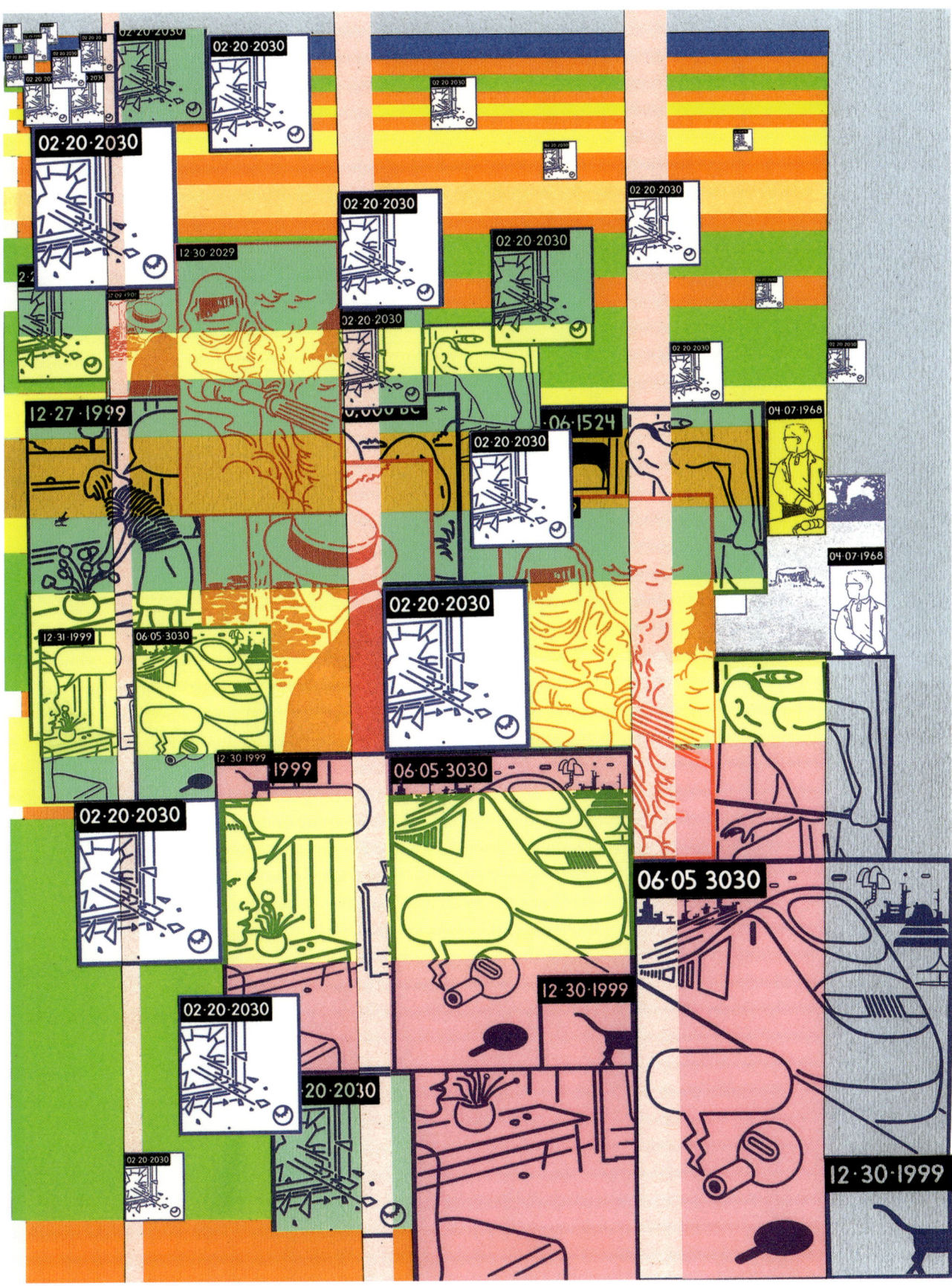

2000

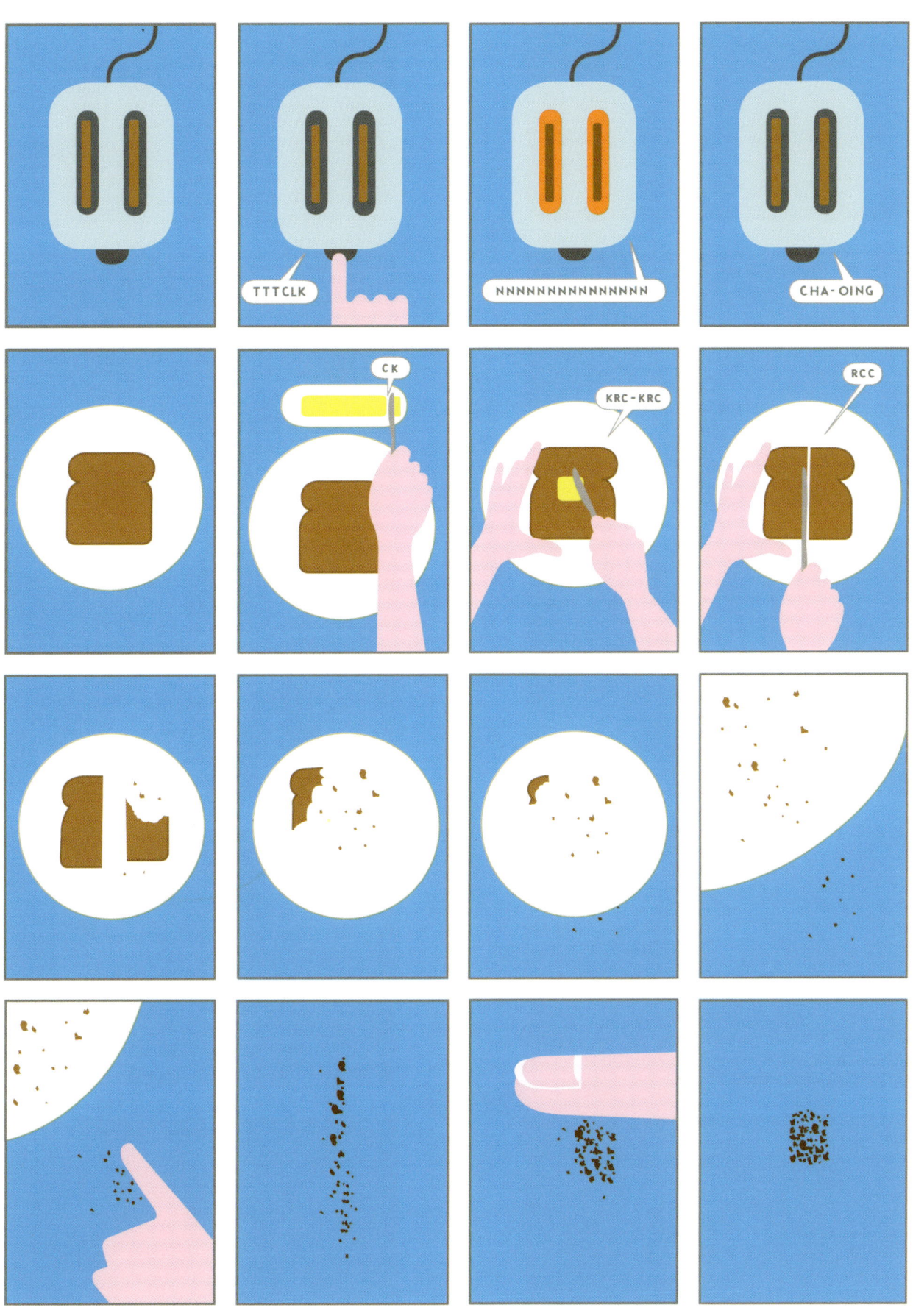

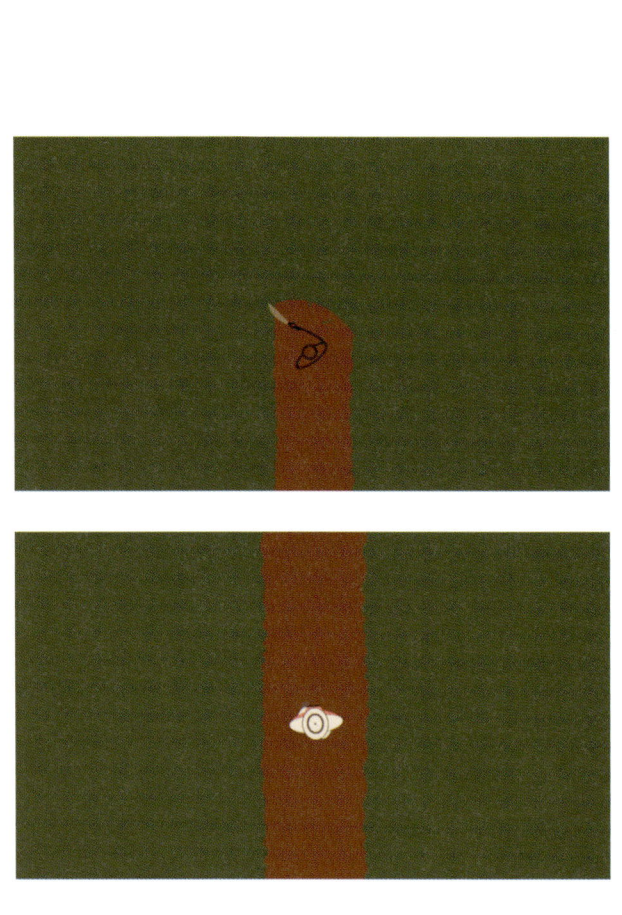
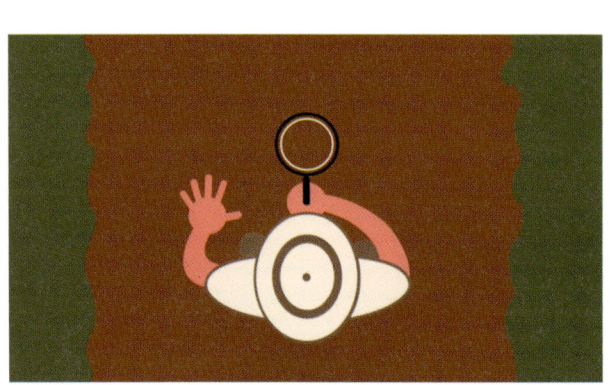

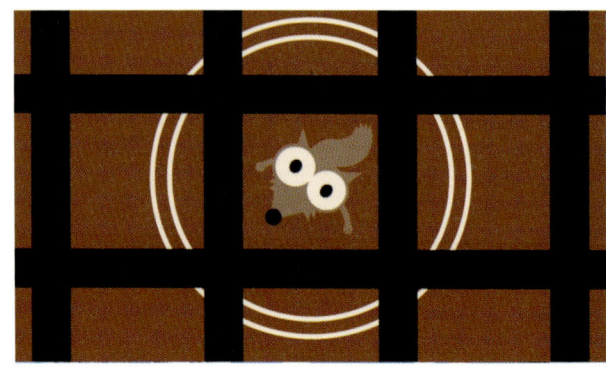

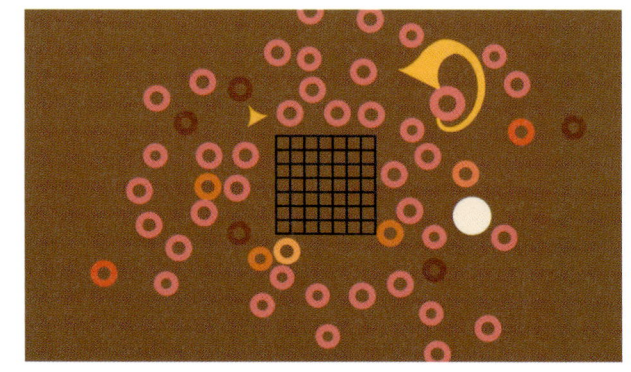
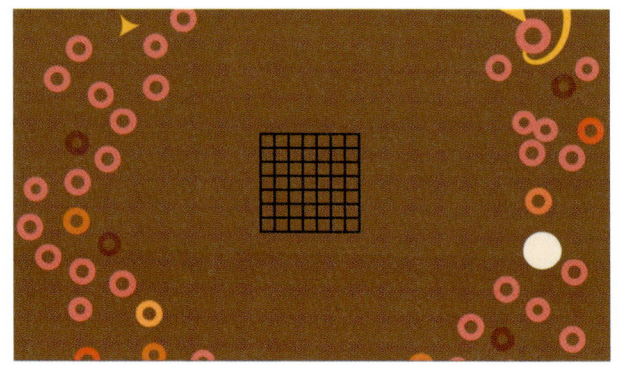

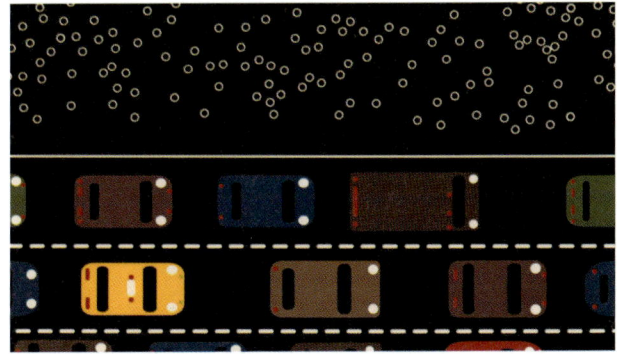
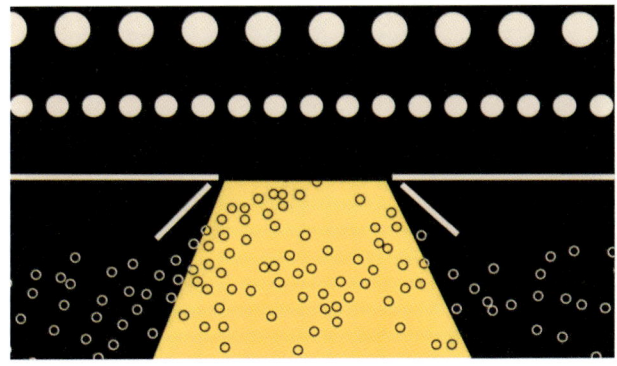
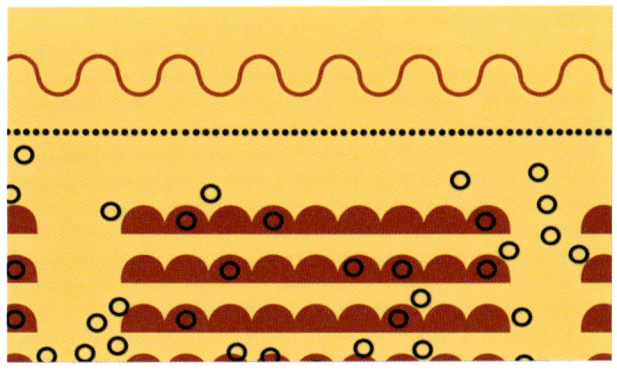
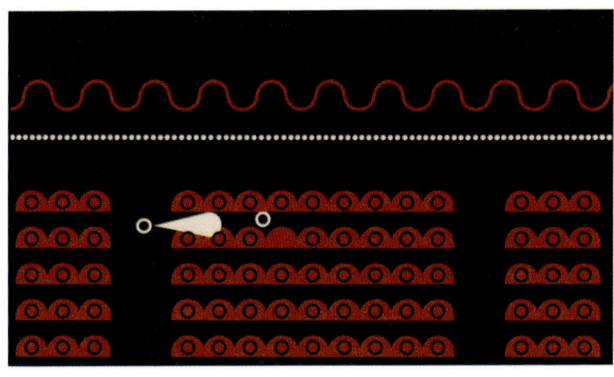
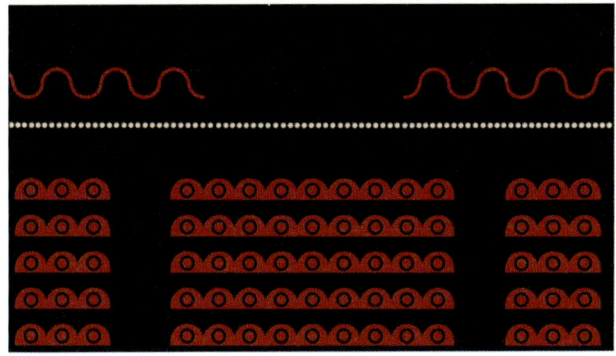

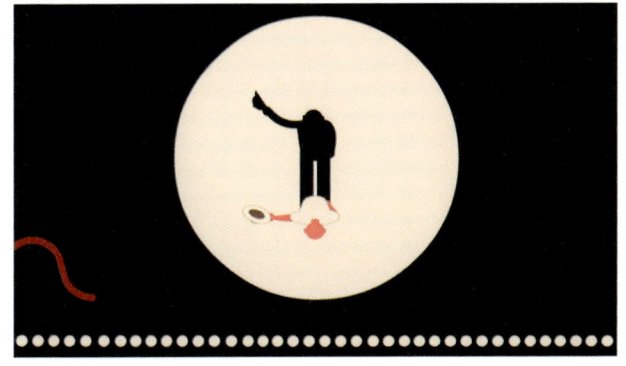
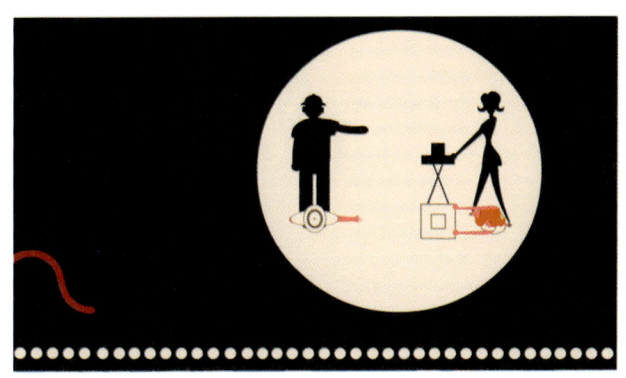

2003

1997

2004

2008

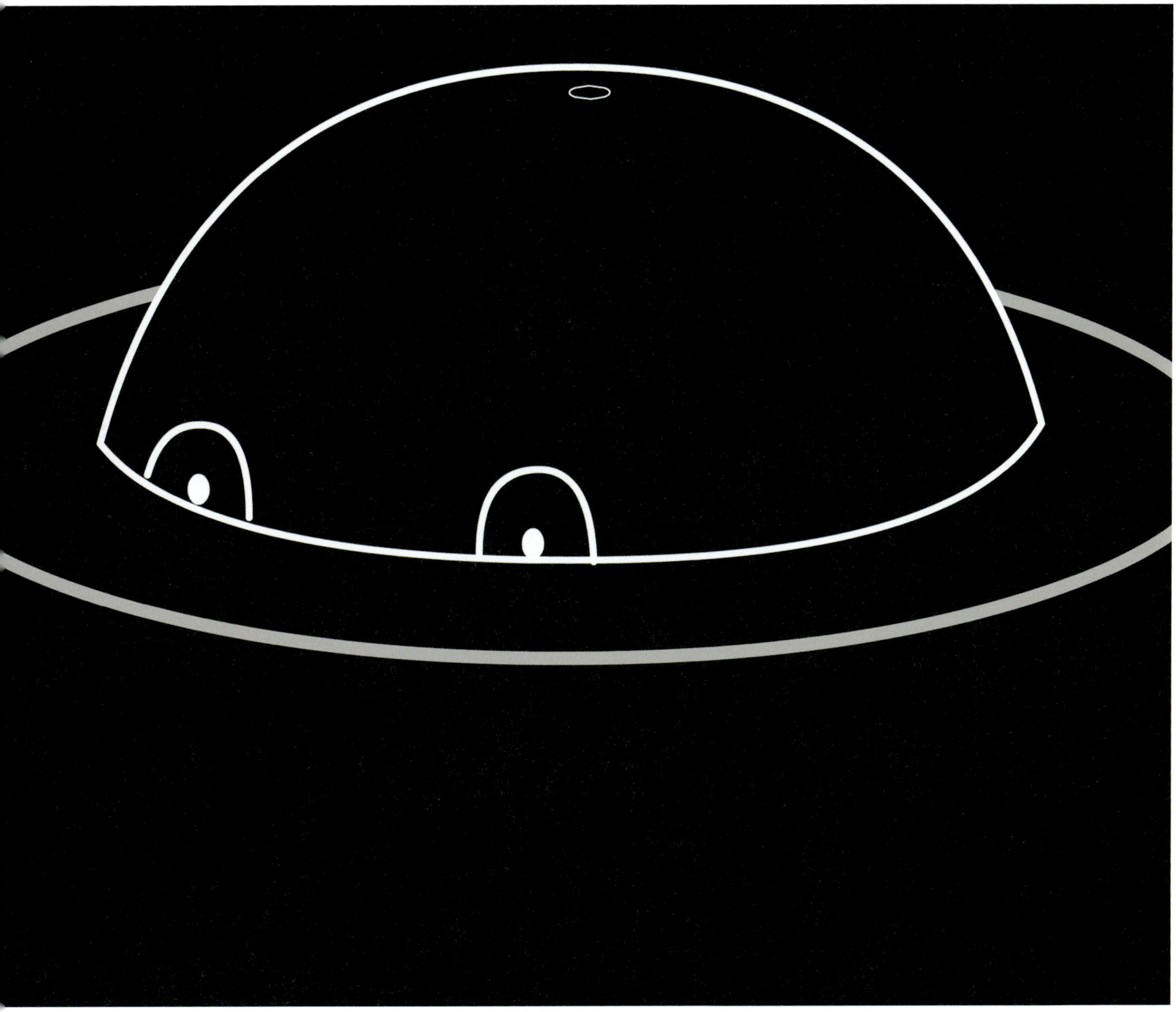

1999

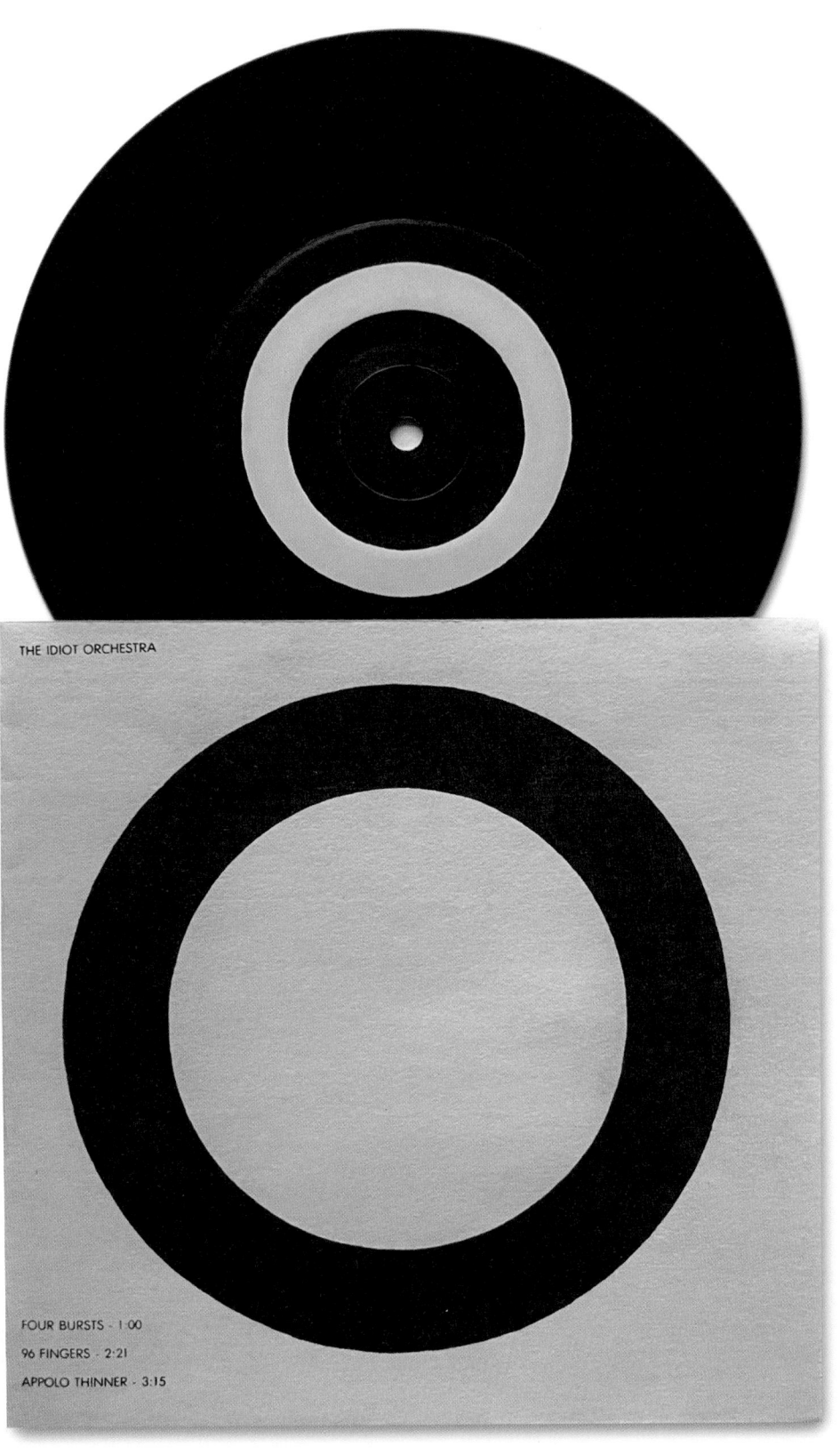

1980

2021

2018

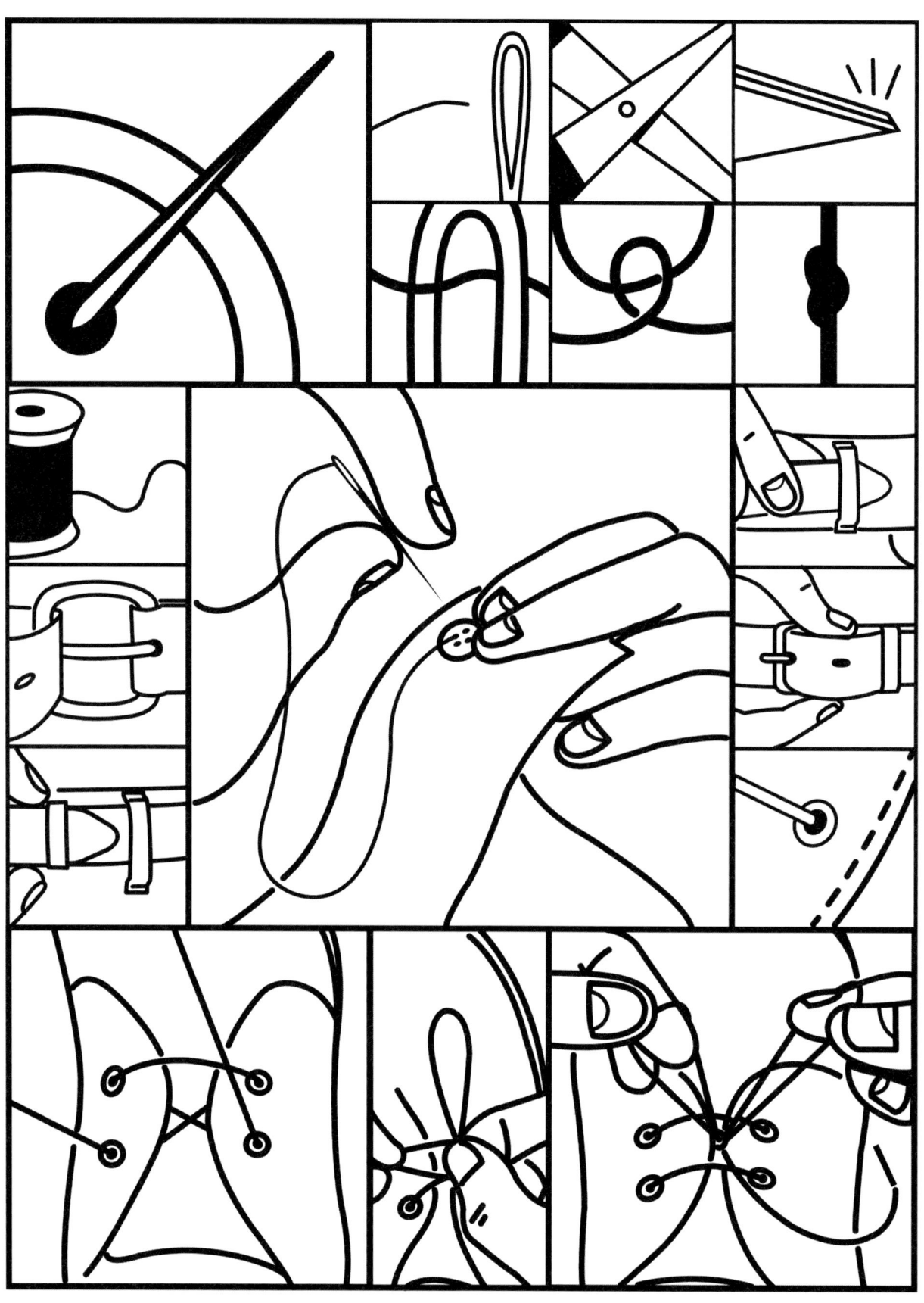

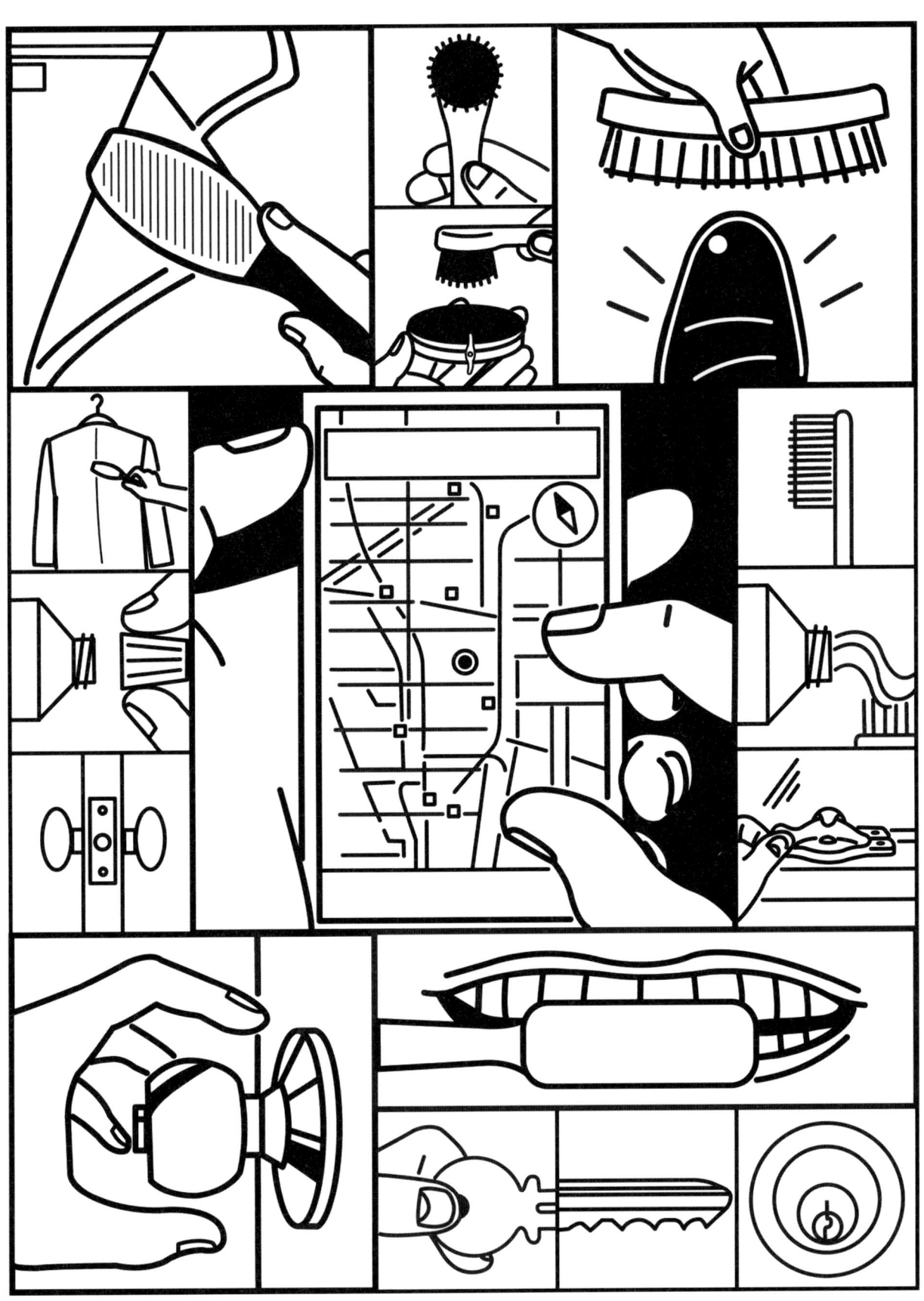

2014

1999

2013

2021

128

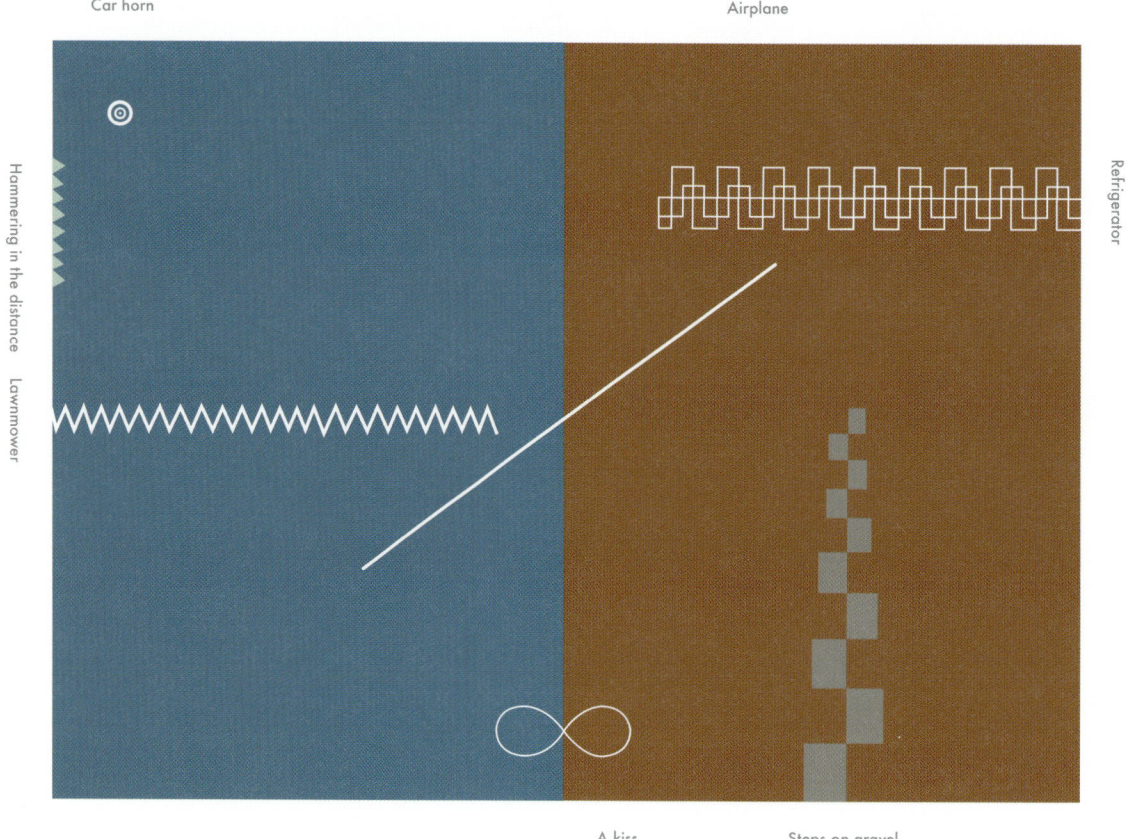

2021

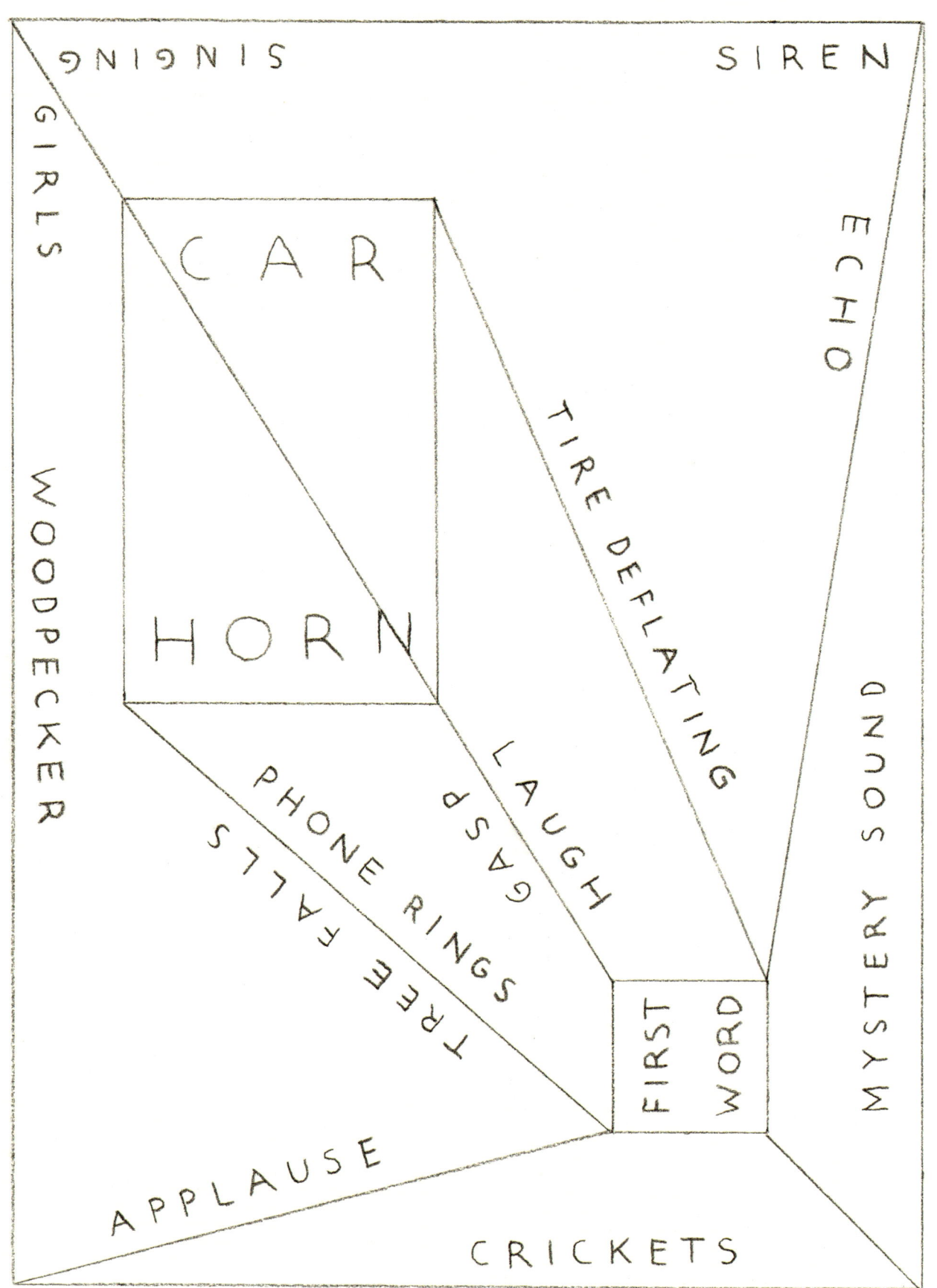

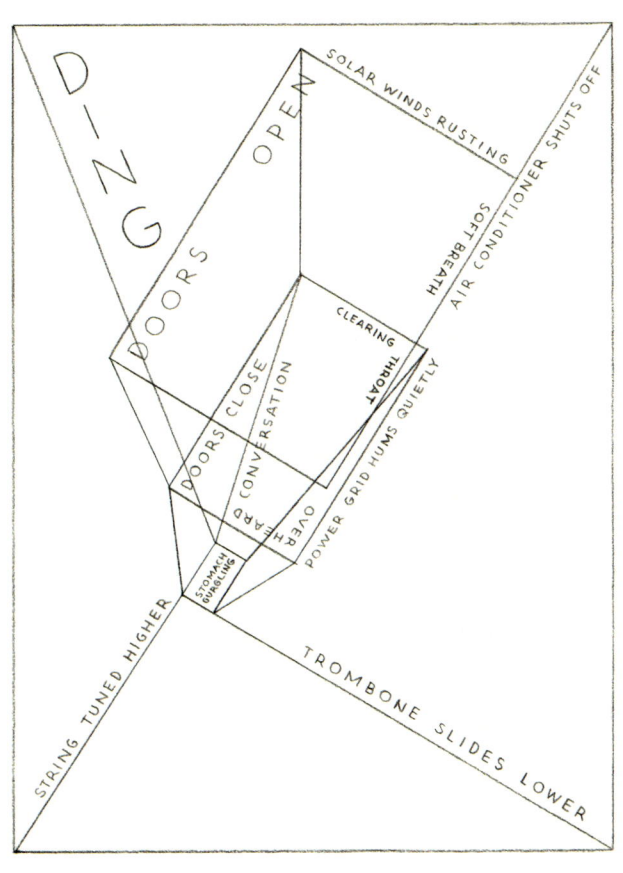
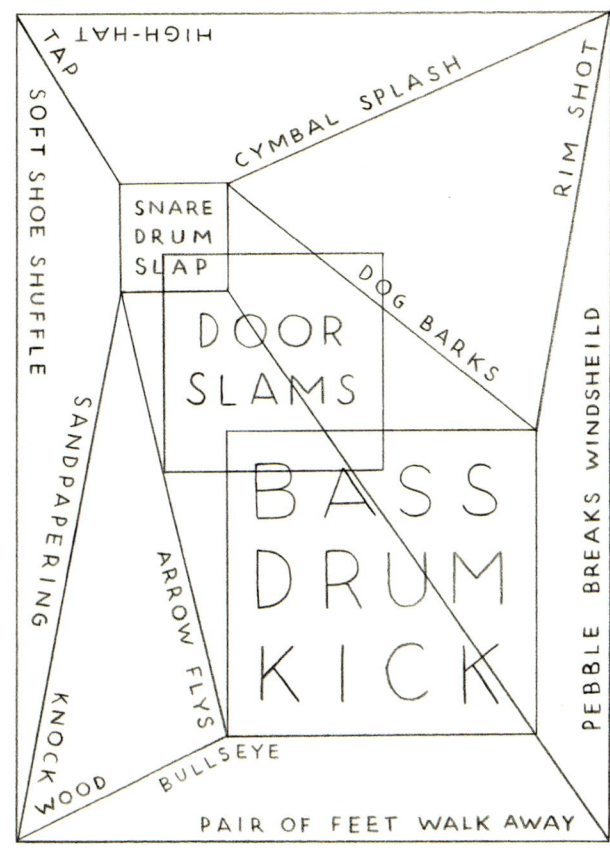
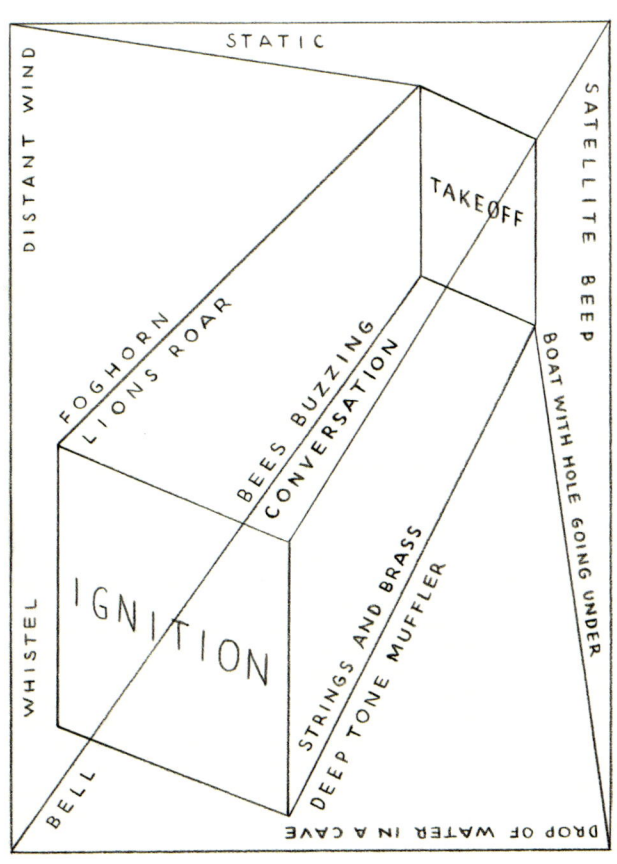
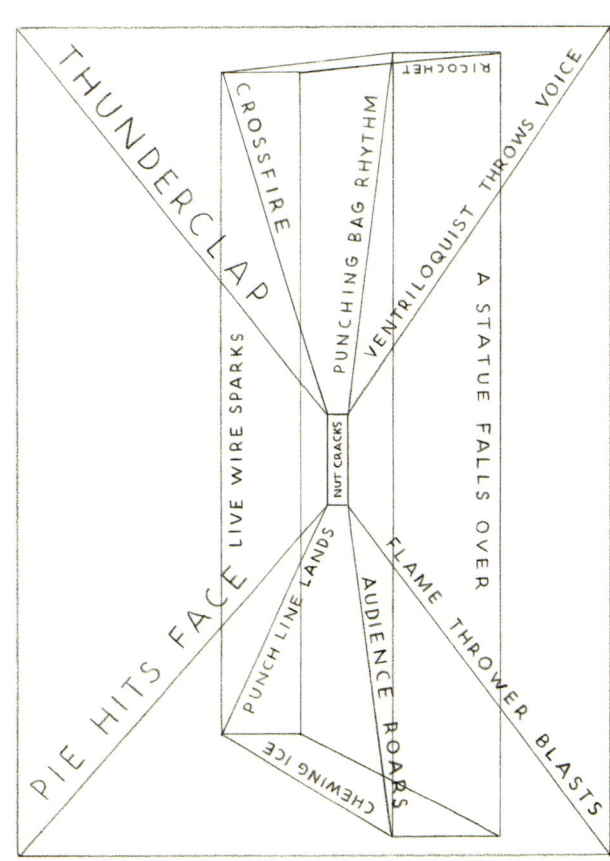

2022

2022

2024

Pages			
4	*Blind Man*, wood, nails, enamel paint, glue / Holz, Nägel, Emailfarbe, Leim, 1965.	34	*Popeye & Olive*, silkscreen on raw canvas / Siebdruck auf Rohleinwand, 182.88 x 182.88 cm, 2019.
7	*Ixnae Nix, Hum of Human Instinct* (1980) and the artist / und der Künstler, St. Mark's Place, New York, May/Mai 1980. Photo/Foto: Julie Wilson.	35	*Popeye and Olive*, book cover / Buchumschlag, published by / herausgegeben von Fotokino, 2023, originally published by / ursprünglich herausgegeben von Editions Cornelius, 2001.
25	*Here/Hier*, silkscreen print / Siebdruck, edition of / Auflage von 100, 30.5 x 30.5 cm, published by / herausgegeben von Desert Island, 2014.	36–37	*Popeye and Olive*, published by / herausgegeben von Fotokino, 2023.
26	*Liquid Liquid*, EP sketch / EP-Skizze, pencil on paper / Bleistift auf Papier, 30.5 x 30.5 cm, 1981.	38	*Popeye*, bust/Büste, wood/Holz, edition of / Auflage von 3, 2015.
27	*Liquid Liquid*, printed record sleeve / gedruckte Plattenhülle, 30.5 x 30.5 cm, 99 Records, 1981.	39	*Popeye and Olive*, woodblock prints / Holzschnittdrucke, published by / herausgegeben von The Arm, 2023.
28–29	*Ixnae Nix, Through My Open Mouth*, street drawing / Strassenzeichnung. Photo/Foto: Martha Fishkin, 1979.	40	*Puzzlehead*, box lid / Schachteldeckel, McGuire Toys, 1990. Sketch on graph paper / Skizze auf Millimeterpapier, 1990.
30	*Ixnae Nix, Holes and Corners*, stencil, spray paint, crayon / Schablone, Sprayfarbe, Wachskreide, 61 x 91.4 cm, 1980.	41	*Puzzlehead*, painted wooden puzzle / bemaltes Holzpuzzle, McGuire Toys, 1990. Promotional postcard / Werbepostkarte, 1990.
31	*Ixnae Nix, Soon As This Is Over*, stencil, spray paint, crayon / Schablone, Sprayfarbe, Wachskreide, 91.4 x 61 cm, 1980; *Ixnae Nix, Different Nervous Rhythms*, stencil, spray paint, crayon / Schablone, Sprayfarbe, Wachskreide, 60.96 x 45.72 cm, 1981; *Ixnae Nix, Incident Instantly Becomes Memory*, street drawing / Strassenzeichnung, 60.9 x 45.7 cm. Photo/Foto: Martha Fishkin, 1979.	42–43	*Go Fish* card game / Kartenspiel, McGuire Toys, 1991. Reissued in / Neuauflage 2016 by/ von Chronicle Books, packaged in a tin box / verpackt in einer Blechdose.
		44	*The Thinkers*, first appeared in the magazine / erstmals erschienen im Magazin RAW #3 volume 2, 1990.
		45	*Uncle Tungsten*, sketch for / Skizze für The New York Times Book Review, 2001.
32	*Ixnae Nix, Constantly Waiting For Someone*, street drawing / Strassenzeichnung. Photo/Foto: Martha Fishkin, 1979; *Ixnae Nix, Watching Her Lips Move*, street drawing / Strassenzeichnung. Photo/Foto: Martha Fishkin, 1979.	46	*Architecture and Disjunction*, illustration for / Illustration für The New York Times Book Review, pen and ink on paper / Kugelschreiber und Tinte auf Papier, 1994.
		47	*Noise Upstairs*, spot series / Spot-Serie, magazine/Magazin The New Yorker, 2012.
33	*Ixnae Nix, Sudden Anatomy*, 218.4 x 134.6 cm, stencil, spray paint, acrylic paint on rolls of paper / Schablone, Spray- und Acrylfarbe auf Papierrollen, 1980.	48	*Liquid Idiot*, record sleeve / Plattenhülle, 1978.

49	*Liquid Liquid Club 57*, collage and Letraset type / Collage und Abreibebuchstaben, artwork for poster / Plakatvorlage, 1981.
50	*Children's Books*, illustration for / Illustration für *The New York Times Book Review*, color paper and twine collage / Farbpapier und Schnurcollage, 2000.
51	*Seeing in the Dark*, illustration for / Illustration für *The New York Times Book Review*, 2002.
52	*Night*, illustration for the magazine / Illustration für das Magazin *The New Yorker*, 2005.
53	*Peur(s) du Noir*, cover for the magazine / Titelseite für das Magazin *Strapazin*, 2007.
54–55	*Peur(s) du Noir*, frames from the animated film / Einzelbilder aus dem Animationsfilm, produced by / produziert von Prima Linea, 2007.
56	*Night becomes Day*, book dummy / Buchmodell, gouache and pencil on paper / Gouache und Farbstift auf Papier, 19 x 23.19 cm, 32 pages/Seiten, 1994.
57	*Happy New Year*, cover illustration for double issue of / Titelblattillustration für eine Doppelausgabe des Magazins *The New Yorker*, 1993–94.
58	*Mofungo, Liquid Liquid, Y-Pants at CBGB*, Letraset type and pinstripe tape on paper / Abreibebuchstaben und schmales Klebeband auf Papier, artwork for poster / Plakatvorlage, 1981.
59	*ESG, Liquid Liquid at Hurrah*, Letraset type, pinstripe tape and collage / Abreibebuchstaben, schmales Klebeband und Collage, artwork for poster / Plakatvorlage, 1980.
60	*Touring*, spot series / Spot-Serie, magazine/Magazin *The New Yorker*, pen and ink on paper / Kugelschreiber und Tinte auf Papier, 21.6 x 27.9 cm, 2009.
61	*Sharing Thoughts*, spot series / Spot-Serie, magazine/Magazin *The New Yorker*, 2013.
62	*Weightless Swatch*, Swatch, multiple sketches / mehrere Skizzen, pencil and markers on printout / Bleistift und Marker auf Ausdruck, detail photo / Detailfoto, 1996.
63	*EO the Solar Toy*, pencil sketch and offset printed instruction page / Bleistiftskizze und in Offset gedruckte Anleitungsseite. Paper tube, offset printed die-cut figure, wood and cardboard base, motor and solar cells / Papierröhre, in Offset bedruckte Stanzfigur, Sockel aus Holz und Karton, Motor und Solarzellen, 1992.
64–65	*The Orange Book*, 23.19 x 23.19 cm, 32 pages/Seiten, published by / herausgegeben von Rizzoli, 1992.
66–67	*My Things*, 10-page visual essay commissioned by / 10-seitiges visuelles Essay im Auftrag von The Aldrich Museum, for the catalog from the exhibition / für den Katalog zur Ausstellung *The Domestic Plane: New Perspectives On Tabletop Art*, 2018.
68	*Memoir*, illustration for / Illustration für *The New York Times Book Review*, 2002.
69	*Strip Turnhout*, poster/Plakat, 2007.
70–71	*Comic Art*, magazine/Magazin, 2007.
72	*Inroads 150 Mercer, Ut and Liquid Idiot*, pen, ink, Letraset type and pinstripe tape on paper / Kugelschreiber, Tinte, Abreibebuchstaben und schmales Klebeband auf Papier, artwork for poster / Plakatvorlage, 1980.
73	*This Side Up*, magazine/Magazin *The New Yorker*, 2020.
74	*Liquid Idiot at A's*, offset/Offsetdruck, 35.5 x 43.2 cm, 1980, *Konk vs. Liquid Liquid*, silkscreen/Siebdruck, 43.2 x 55.8 cm, 1981.
75	*Bellhead*, 12" single / 12-Inch-Single, DFA Records, 2024.

76	*Süddeutsche Zeitung, Feuilleton* Grossformat, offset/Offsetdruck, 2016.
77–79	*Here/Hier*, pages/Seiten 2 & 3, ink on vellum / Tinte auf Pergament, edited pages were published in *RAW* magazine / die bearbeiteten Seiten wurden im Magazin ‹RAW› herausgegeben, 1989.
80–81	*Here Remix*, two of four pages / zwei von vier Seiten, inkjet printed on color paper / Tintenstrahldruck auf Farbpapier, collaged/collagiert, 2000.
82	*The Elimination of Reality Through Difference*, commissioned print series by / Auftragsdruckserie von White Columns, edition of / Auflage von 50, each print unique / jeder Druck ist ein Unikat, Risograph, 2021.
83	*Bird's Eye View BBQ*, magazine/Magazin *The New Yorker*, 2002.
84–85	*ctrl*, two of six pages / zwei von sechs Seiten, published in / herausgegeben in *McSweeney's Quarterly Concern #13*, 2004.
86–87	*Micro Loup*, frames for the animated film / Einzelbilder für den Animationsfilm, 7 min./Min., produced by / produziert von Prima Linea, 2003.
88	*Swim Swam Swum*, magazine/Magazin *The New Yorker*, 2008.
89	*Modern Art*, magazine/Magazin *The New Yorker*, 2005.
90	*Dream Vacation*, magazine/Magazin *The New Yorker*, 2020.
91	*Summer Reading*, illustration for / Illustration für *The New York Times Book Review*, 2002.
92	*La Méridienne*, book cover illustration / Illustration für den Buchumschlag, published by / herausgegeben von Robert Laffont, 1997.
93	*Pricing & Ethical Guidelines Handbook*, book cover illustration / Illustration für den Buchumschlag, published by / herausgegeben von Graphic Artist Guild, 2007.
94	*Ninety-Five Fools*, pencil sketch on paper / Farbstiftskizze auf Papier, magazine/Magazin *The New Yorker*, 1995.
95	*What's Wrong With This Book?*, 23.19 x 23.19 cm, 32 pages/Seiten, published by / herausgegeben von Viking Penguin, 1997.
96	*Cat 'n' Mouse*, magazine/Magazin *The New Yorker*, 2004.
97	*Noise New York*, magazine/Magazin *The New Yorker*, 2019.
98–99	Liquid Liquid, *Slip In and Out of Phenomenon*, 3-disc set with booklet and bonus CD / 3-Disc-Set mit Booklet und Bonus-CD, Domino Records UK, 2008.
100	Liquid Liquid, *Optimo*, 12" EP / 12-Inch-EP, 99 Records, 1983.
101	Liquid Liquid, *Collected Tracks 1981–1984*. LP sleeve design / Design der LP-Hülle, 2023.
102–103	*Try*, willingtotry.com, an animated interactive website for a Japanese education company / eine animierte interaktive Website für ein japanisches Bildungsunternehmen, 1999.
104–105	*The Idiot Orchestra*, 7" record / 7-Inch-Schallplatte, offset sleeve and labels / in Offset gedruckte Plattenhülle und Etiketten, self-published / Selbstveröffentlichung, 1980.
106–107	*Cement Shoe*, created for / geschaffen für *The Shoo Show*, Anton Kern Window, cement/Zement, 2021.
108–109	*The Way There and Back*, an installation of 62 shoe-shaped sculptures / eine Installation von 60 schuhförmigen Skulpturen, various materials / verschiedene Materialien, 2018.

110–111	*My Things*, 2 pages of a 10-page visual essay commissioned by / 2 Seiten eines 10-seitigen visuellen Essays im Auftrag von The Aldrich Museum, for the catalog from the exhibition / für den Katalog zur Ausstellung *The Domestic Plane: New Perspectives on Tabletop Art*, 2018.	130–131	*Listen*, various pages from the book / verschiedene Seiten aus dem Buch, published by / herausgegeben von Fotokino, 2021.
112–115	*Here/Hier*, pages from the graphic novel / Seiten aus der Graphic Novel, 300 pages/Seiten, published by / herausgegeben von Pantheon, 2014.	132	*Car Horn*, sound drawing series / Serie von Klangzeichnungen, pencil on paper / Bleistift auf Papier, 22.9 x 30.5 cm, 2022.
116–117	*Here/Hier*, various preparation sketches / verschiedene Vorbereitungsskizzen, pencil, watercolor, inkjet, collage / Farbstift, Wasserfarbe, Tintenstrahl, Collage, 2013.	133	*Ding*, pencil on paper / Bleistift auf Papier, 22.8 x 30.5 cm, 2023; *Bass Drum Kick*, pencil on paper / Bleistift auf Papier, 22.8 x 30.5 cm, 2022; *Ignition*, pencil on paper / Bleistift auf Papier, 22.8 x 30.5 cm, 2022. *Thunderclap*, pencil on paper / Bleistift auf Papier, 22.8 x 30.5 cm, 2023.
118–119	*Here/Hier*, various pages from the graphic novel / verschiedene Seiten aus der Graphic Novel, published by / herausgegeben von Pantheon, 2014.	134	*Ah Choo*, pencil on paper / Bleistift auf Papier, 22.8 x 30.5 cm, 2023.
120–121	*Here/Hier*, various preparation sketches / verschiedene Vorbereitungsskizzen, pencil, inkjet / Bleistift, Farbstift, Tintenstrahl, 2013.	135	*Rain Stops*, pencil on paper / Bleistift auf Papier, 22.8 x 30.5 cm, 2023.
122–123	*Here/Hier*, various pages from the graphic novel / verschiedene Seiten aus der Graphic Novel, published by / herausgegeben von Pantheon, 2014.	136	*Echo*, laser-cut steel letters, carbon rods, shadow / lasergeschnittene Stahlbuchstaben, Karbonstangen, Schatten, 2024.
124–125	*Here/Hier*, various pages from the graphic novel / verschiedene Seiten aus der Graphic Novel, published by / herausgegeben von Pantheon, 2014.		
126–127	*Listen*, digital drawing for an edition of 30 silkscreen prints / digitale Zeichnung für eine Auflage von 30 Siebdrucken, printed by / gedruckt von Frédéric Béjean at / in der Villa Belleville, Paris (gray-blue version / grau-blaue Version), published by / herausgegeben von Fotokino, 2021.		
128–129	*Bird Songs*, various frames taken from animated interstitials created for / verschiedene Einzelbilder aus Kurzanimationen zwischen den Programmen geschaffen für Canal+ TV, 2003.		

Anette Gehrig has been director and curator of Cartoonmuseum Basel – Centre for Narrative Art since 2008. She has curated exhibitions with Aline Kominsky-Crumb & Robert Crumb, Blutch, Catherine Meurisse, Christoph Niemann, Joe Sacco, Chris Ware and Joost Swarte, among others, and is also an editor of publications. The exhibitions at Cartoonmuseum Basel address the full spectrum of narrative art and touch on related fields, such as animation and fine art.

•

Vincent Tuset-Anrès has been the artistic director of Fotokino (Marseille) since 2004. He has curated numerous exhibitions with artists such as Paul Cox, Nathalie Du Pasquier, Philippe Weisbecker, Jochen Gerner, Yto Barrada, Atak and Kitty Crowther. He is also a graphic designer and runs the Fotokino publishing house. In 2021, he invited Richard McGuire to exhibit at Studio Fotokino and has since published several books with him.

Anette Gehrig ist seit 2008 Direktorin und Kuratorin am Cartoonmuseum Basel – Zentrum für narrative Kunst. Sie kuratierte Ausstellungen mit Aline Kominsky-Crumb & Robert Crumb, Blutch, Catherine Meurisse, Christoph Niemann, Joe Sacco, Chris Ware, Joost Swarte und anderen. Daneben ist sie Herausgeberin von Publikationen. Die Ausstellungen im Cartoonmuseum Basel widmen sich der gesamten Bandbreite der narrativen Kunst und berühren verwandte Gebiete wie Animation und freie Kunst.

•

Vincent Tuset-Anrès ist seit 2004 künstlerischer Leiter von Fotokino (Marseille). Er hat zahlreiche Ausstellungen mit Künstlern wie Paul Cox, Nathalie Du Pasquier, Philippe Weisbecker, Jochen Gerner, Yto Barrada, Atak und Kitty Crowther kuratiert. Er ist auch Grafikdesigner und leitet den Fotokino-Verlag. Im Jahr 2021 lud er Richard McGuire ein, im Studio Fotokino auszustellen, und hat seitdem mehrere Bücher mit ihm veröffentlicht.

Bibliographic information published by the Deutsche Nationalbibliothek: The Deutsche Nationalbibliothek lists this publication in the Deutsche Nationalbibliografie; detailed bibliographic data is available on the Internet at http://dnb.dnb.de.

Bibliografische Information der Deutschen Nationalbibliothek: Die Deutsche Nationalbibliothek verzeichnet diese Publikation in der Deutschen Nationalbibliografie; detaillierte bibliografische Daten sind im Internet über http://dnb.dnb.de abrufbar.

© 2024 Christoph Merian Verlag
© 2024 Texts/Texte: Authors/ Autoren: Richard McGuire, Vincent Tuset-Anrès, Anette Gehrig
© 2024 Works/Werke: Richard McGuire

Pages/Seiten 17, 18, 48, 52, 57, 60, 61, 73, 83, 88, 89, 90, 94, 96, 97: © Richard McGuire & *The New Yorker*. Used by permission / Verwendet mit Genehmigung. All rights reserved / Alle Rechte vorbehalten.

Page/Seite 106–107: photo/Foto © Dan Bradica, courtesy of / mit freundlicher Genehmigung von Anton Kern Gallery.

Page/Seite 33: photo/Foto © Jean Vong, courtesy of / mit freundlicher Genehmigung von MoMA.

All rights reserved; no part of this publication may be reproduced, stored in a retrieval system or transmitted in any form or by any means, electronic, mechanical, photocopying, recording or otherwise, without prior written permission from the publisher.

Alle Rechte vorbehalten; kein Teil dieses Werkes darf in irgendeiner Form ohne vorherige schriftliche Genehmigung des Verlags reproduziert oder unter Verwendung elektronischer Systeme verarbeitet, vervielfältigt oder verbreitet werden.

merianverlag.ch

Editor and project management / Herausgeberin und Projektleitung
Cartoonmuseum Basel – Centre for Narrative Art / Zentrum für narrative Kunst, Anette Gehrig

Conception / Konzept
Richard McGuire, Vincent Tuset-Anrès

Texts / Texte
Richard McGuire, Vincent Tuset-Anrès, Anette Gehrig

Graphic design, lithography / Grafische Gestaltung, Lithografie
Vincent Tuset-Anrès, Marseille

Translation and editorial reading in English and German / Übersetzung und Lektorat Englisch und Deutsch
Simon and Ruth Thomas, Lyon

Printed by / Druck
CCI, Marseille

Typeface / Schrift
Futura Now

Paper / Papier
Fedrigoni Sirio color iris 290 g/m² (cover/Umschlag),
Sirio color vermiglione 290 g/m²,
Sirio color perla 140 g/m²,
Symbol tatami white 135 g/m²,
Woodstock giallo 140 g/m²

Acknowledgments

I wish to express my deepest thanks to Anette Gehrig, director of Cartoonmuseum Basel – Centre for Narrative Art, and Vincent Tuset-Anrès, director of Fotokino in Marseille, for making this exhibition and catalog possible. I would also like to thank Mia Fineman and Joel Smith for their generous loan of artwork.

Ich möchte Anette Gehrig, Direktorin des Cartoonmuseums Basel – Zentrum für narrative Kunst, und Vincent Tuset-Anrès, Direktor von Fotokino in Marseille, für die Ermöglichung dieser Ausstellung und dieses Katalogs meinen tiefsten Dank aussprechen. Weiter möchte ich Mia Fineman und Joel Smith für ihre grosszügige Leihgabe von Kunstwerken danken.

Richard McGuire

ISBN 978-3-03969-024-4